My PFP

Is New Member's Class Necessary?

FRANKLIN L. ELMORE

ISBN 978-1-0980-1018-8 (paperback)
ISBN 978-1-0980-1019-5 (digital)

Christian Faith Publishing, Inc.
832 Park Avenue
Meadville, PA 16335
www.christianfaithpublishing.com

Scriptures marked (KJV) are taken from the KING JAMES VERSION (KJV): KING JAMES VERSION, public domain.

Scriptures marked (NASB) are taken from the NEW AMERICAN STANDARD BIBLE®, Copyright © 1960, 1962, 1963, 1968, 1971, 1972, 1973, 1975, 1977, 1995 by The Lockman Foundation. Used by permission."

Printed in the United States of America

The practical application of the "Word of God changes lives."

—Rev. Franklin L. Elmore

Contents

CHAPTER 1

My PFP

What are the practical foundational principles that fuel your biblical hermeneutics?

Hopefully, by the end of this book, you should be able to say emphatically that you know your own PFP. Being led by the Holy Spirit, I've learned that we must digest and regurgitate the truth. God gives us information (wisdom) to deal with our own situation and circumstances. Sometimes, he allows us to share that illumination with others. Never have I preached or taught a sermon or lesson without first applying the message to my life.

"The husbandman that laboureth must be first partaker of the fruits" (2 Timothy 2:6, KJV). This is what I believe in. What you believe should not be based on something you read. It should be based on what you experienced to be true. For instance, I walked into a church one day. The atmosphere was electric. The praise and laughter was as a roaring lion. The choir sang as angels. The preacher preached like the Apostle Paul. I felt something drawing me to become part of that ministry. Yet I knew nothing about their doctrine. Before the pastor took his text, he lifted up his Bible and asked the congregation to repeat after him their positive confession of faith:

"This is my Bible. I am what it says I am. I can do what it says I can do. I am a believer and not a doubter. And my life is better after hearing the word of faith 'cause faith cometh by hearing and hearing by the Word of God." Somebody shouted *halleluiah!*

I read their beliefs or creed on the back of the morning program. The questions remained, *Do I believe the same things? Or do I understand what it means?* It read, We Believe.

1. We believe in the triune God who exists as God the Father, the Son, and the Holy Spirit (1 John 5:7).
2. Jesus Christ is true God and true man (John 1:1–4).
3. The Holy Spirit is a person in the Godhead and God's agent in the world (Romans 8:26; John 14:17, 26; John 16:7).
4. The Old and New Testament Scriptures are the divinely inspired Word of God (2 Timothy 3:16).
5. All have sinned and come short of the glory of God and are in need of salvation (Romans 3:23).
6. Salvation has been provided for all men through the death and resurrection of Jesus Christ (Romans 10:9).
7. It is the will of God that every believer becomes filled with the Holy Spirit (Ephesians 5:17–21).
8. Healing is provided in the redemptive work of Christ and is available to every believer (Isaiah 53:5).
9. The ministry consists of all those who received Jesus Christ as Lord (Matthew 10:40).
10. There shall be a bodily resurrection of the just and the unjust (1 Corinthians 15:51–58).
11. The return of Jesus Christ will be personal and visible (1 Thessalonians 4:13–18).
12. We believe the doctrines of the ministry ordained by Jesus are water baptism and observance of the Lord's Supper (Acts 2:38; Galatians 3:27; 1 Corinthians 11:23–30).

Like most new converts or relocating Christians, church doctrine are not always immediately available. Sometimes, there is no way of knowing whether or not our actions contradict a doctrine until we commit an offense. New Christians are less likely to accept the chastisement of an elder or mother of the church like a relocating Christian. This is one of the reasons why a new member's class is necessary in every ministry.

The development of *My Practical Foundational Principles* (PFP) can be attributed to my past ministry experiences and infirmities God has brought me through. I would like to mention a few of the life experiences that has shaped *My PFP*.

My ministry experiences began in 1991 in a small town called Paducah, Kentucky. It is located about 370 miles south of Chicago, Illinois. It has the Ohio River flowing on its banks. The black population in Paducah was 10 percent of the total Metropolitan area of one hundred thousand people. Black people stayed on their side of the track. It was a city that shared southern values.

The ministry I would like to mention is the church I was baptized in by Rev. Charles Staples. It moved over the years from 8th Street Tabernacle Baptist Church to 9th Street Tabernacle Baptist Church. It was 1991 when I returned home to my mother's church to begin my Christian journey as a preacher of the gospel of Jesus Christ. Thinking that the church was a utopian society after living in sin for ten years, I was sadly mistaken.

Upon joining the local church, it was as if the fourth grade failure syndrome had returned to my life. The newly elected pastor, Rev. Turner, welcomed me as a member. He informed me that my calling to preach should not be made known to the congregation at the time. He began teaching me early how to mentor young preachers without knowing it.

One Sunday, the pastor was out-of-town. He left me instructions not to tell anyone about our conversation. He also asked me not to do anything. I interpreted that to mean not teach or preach. So that Sunday morning, Deacon Baker asked me to open the morning worship service with prayer. Growing up in the church, I could sometimes repeat verbatim what Deacon Tally would pray. Needless to say, I was very familiar with kneeling on one knee with my face in the pew to pray. I prayed, and the congregation was graceful afterward.

That afternoon, the pastor called me and told me that he was disappointed in me. I asked what I had done, thinking I had offended someone or transgressed a church doctrine. He said he told me not to do anything. I had no idea he meant praying openly in the church during devotion. He never told the church I had accepted my call to preach the gospel. However, he allowed me to teach children's church during morning worship services.

After seven months, I was led by the Holy Spirit to leave the church for St. Louis where I would begin my public ministry. So on my last Sunday, the pastor announced that I would be leaving for seminary training. He allowed me to pray during altar call during morning service. I learned that young ministers need someone to listen, believe, and watch to see if they have been called. I found that a man's gift will make room for him.

In my next ministry in St. Louis, Mo, taught me a lot about spiritual ministry. I left Paducah, Kentucky, and relocated in St. Louis, Mo, in 1992. My living conditions were horrid. I was renting a converted six-by-six bathroom on the third floor. I felt God was punishing me for my backsliding for ten years. So I endured as a good soldier. I began my public ministry. I was accepted as a preacher of the gospel.

However, I was not allowed to preach on a Sunday morning during worship service. The pastor, William Jones, informed me that the congregation did not come to see me. According to him, the congregation could only receive from him. I accepted that idea as a novice. I was allowed to preach with others during evening services or special programs.

I found out that the fear of the pastor was that his ministry would be destroyed from the inside. He based this on William Seymour of Azusa Street ministry in California. I was, however, given the opportunity to attend a non-accredited Christian College program.

Eventually, I was given the opportunity to teach several classes voluntarily. Humility was my lesson during the three years of ministry working as building custodian, director of bookstore, television program editor, blue chip camera operator, and informal college instructor. I was experiencing a personal issue with my wife of one year. We decided to divorce. The pastor informed me that if I divorce, I would only be a pew member. He said if I played my cards right, he would look out for me. Well, I divorced.

The next Sunday morning, I found that the doors of the church locks were changed. I was informed by the pastor that my membership was no longer required. It hurts, but I learned valuable lessons about the grace of God. After leaving St. Louis, Mo, I moved to Chicago, Illinois.

In 1996, I joined West Side Christian Center. Rev. Owens was the pastor. During my three years as an associate minister, I learned that trust is a very important factor in the lives of associate ministers. The first two years of working in the ministry was wonderful. I preached on Sunday mornings. I was instrumental in establishing a tape ministry men's fellowship and prayer breakfast. I was ordained as a full gospel minister in 1998. My pastor suffered stroke in the spring of 1998. He was not able to verbally express his thoughts. His wife would type his messages and assist him with reading them. She was not a minister at the time of his stroke. After his stroke, she and her oldest son professed a calling to preach.

So on the same day that I was ordained, she was licensed to preach the gospel. I was not aware of the revenue of the church. We did not have annual meetings to discuss the finances of the church. I found out that the pastor's family owned surrounding property that was netting the church $4,000 per week. Instead of considering me to step in and pastor until someone could be elected, the pastor's wife sent me a letter informing me that if I wanted to continue ministering at that church, I had to be trained by her. She was not ordained, but she managed the finances at home and the church. Her decision made me feel irrelevant and dispensable. It was obvious to me that because I was not family, I would not be trusted to oversee the finances and church business. This experienced led me to ask the question, how does a person minister when they are not trusted?

In 1999, I joined New Community Church with Elder Dan Clifton as the pastor. The church is located on the west side of Chicago, Illinois. I served as an associate minister for three years. I was required to be at the church four days a week. Wednesdays were Bible study, Friday was outreach, Saturday was choir practice, and Sunday morning was worship services. The Scripture that proclaimed "Study to show thyself approved unto God" caused me to consider a formal education.

I was led by the Holy Spirit to go to a formal theology college. I enrolled at Trinity International University in Deerfield, Illinois. My major was Christian Ministry. My studies made it hard for me to be at church four days per week. I left the church to become a full-time student. In 2005, I graduated with a bachelor of arts in Christian ministry. I graduated with honor of cum laude. In 2010, I received a master of arts in urban ministry. I graduated with honor of cum laude.

While in my undergraduate studies, I founded Practical Word Ministries Inc. My membership was made up of my wife's sister and laws and their families. During the first year, I baptized fourteen children. I witnessed a miracle that allowed a child to walk again. My membership grew to over fifty members. I became affiliated with Southern Baptist. In 2013, I returned to New Community Church. The Lord told me to go and help my brother. So I served as an assistant pastor for three years. My duties included director of Christian education. I was responsible for Sunday school, choir, outreach, hospitality, Bible study, and the Lord's Supper.

The pastor was asked by his doctors to retire due to his health. He was facing the possibility of dialysis. Pastor Clifton asked me to accept a greater role of preaching on Sunday mornings. He was unable to stand for extended periods. Pastor Clifton was limited to giving closing remarks. After a year, his health improved. Dialysis was not required. The pastor began fulfilling his responsibilities.

The Lord said to me, "Your work here is done." I learned firsthand that obedience is better than sacrifice. By being obedient to the voice that commanded me to help my brother, I was blessed. Many people wonder if they are in the will of God. Somehow, the Spirit of God will let you know. There are some things we do not have to guess at. We just know that we know. We know when the window of heaven opens up and pours out a blessing that we have to make room to receive it.

In 2005, I began my internship at Soul Reviving Missionary Baptist Church. The pastor was Rev. Larry Linder. The church was located at 9537 S. Perry Ave., Chicago, Illinois. I was working on my bachelor of ministry at trinity International University, Deerfield, Illinois. I chose Pastor Linder to direct my internship because of his passion for education. He once shared with the congregation how he struggled to earn his masters of divinity degree. His wife was a principal at Emanuel Baptist Church, Christian Elementary School, located at 83rd and Damen Ave., Chicago, Illinois. Pastor Linder was also a teacher at the school. I believed he would be sympathetic to my struggles as a young man trying to do something no one in my family had achieved. None of my thirteen siblings graduated from college. I was blessed that my mother who had a third-grade education lived long enough to witness my graduation. During my undergraduate studies, I served the church as a youth director. My internship was a six-month study at Soul Reviving. It was a very educational experience. The church was originally founded by a gospel singing group called The Soul Reviving. Under Pastor Linder, it transformed from an emphasis on music to the Word of God. The membership struggled with the change, especially when the minister of music could play and sing like Mahalia Jackson.

When he was let go, several of the members decided to fellowship at other churches. The pastor was very focused on the vision he had received of the Lord. He was steadfast and unmovable. His faith prevailed.

Hebrews 11:2 (KJV) says, "For by it (faith) the elders obtained a good report." As a youth director, I was given the responsibility of teaching the youth ages twelve to eighteen. I taught on Sundays during Sunday school (boys) and Wednesday Bible study (Coed). The youth were not interested in the syllabus of learning and memorizing Scriptures. I asked the students during Bible study if the church is a learning institution. One suggested that the church is not a learning center because there were no other ethnic group teaching the syllabuses. So I had to develop a relationship with each student in order to reach them. The relationships were not superficial. I made myself available to assist each student even when we were not in class. Eventually, my method became effective.

By the end of the internship, I was able to persuade the congregation to allow their children to go on a fishing trip to Wisconsin with me. Pastor Linder understood what was required during my internship. Unlike other secular internships, I knew that a job was not my objective. I wanted to establish a ministry that would continue long after I had completed my internship. The church's educational department was second to none. What I learned during monthly teachers' meetings enhanced my preparation routines.

As a young man, I did not experience physical infirmities. During my high school years between 1975 and 1978 at Paducah Tilghman High School in Paducah, Kentucky, I participated in football, basketball, and track and field. The only pain I experienced was during practice. My older brother Leroy Elmore told me a story about my family. It was in the fall of 1959 about September 7. He said I was born malnourished. I remained in an incubator at Lourdes Hospital along the Ohio River. The Catholic nuns tried to feed me intravenously without success. I still bear the scars in my thigh where they tried to insert the needles. My family was called together to receive the bad news. My mother, Mary Williams, was told that I would not survive the night. They asked if they could baptize me. She agreed to let them baptize me. According to my siblings that was the last time our family prayed on one accord. The next day, their prayers were answered. I was baptized in a small bowl. When the nuns put me in the water, I was unresponsive. However, when I emerged from the water, I began crying profusely. I went on to become an overweight child with stretch marks to prove it. So I realized that a miracle is possible. That story caused me to think that God has always been with me. It made it easier for me to accept his call for me to preach the gospel message. My mother once told me that because Jesus's bones were never broken on the cross and my bones had never been broken, I was anointed. To some, that may not seem much. But to someone struggling to believe God had called them to preach the gospel, it mattered.

When I was about six years old, I remember my grandfather having his leg amputated. He had diabetes, but insulin was not available in 1965. I never talked about it with my mother. I was not aware of a genetic transference of diseases like diabetes.

In 2006, as an adult, I experienced an infirmity that would change the course of my life. My wife and I had just returned from Las Vegas celebrating her birthday. I felt very different. My mouth was dry even after drinking a glass of water. I went to the restroom every five minutes. My head was pounding like I was being hit over and over again with a sledgehammer. It was Easter Sunday morning when my condition became unbearable. My wife, Arnetha, insisted that my deacons rush me to Trinity Hospital in Chicago, Illinois. The doctor informed my wife that if I had waited two more hours, I could had a stroke or go into a coma and die. My glucose was over six hundred. I had a bleeding pituitary gland in the base of my skull. I had a tumor on my brain and was experiencing an aneurism on my brain. My condition was treated with steroids for the pituitary gland. I received insulin for Type 2 diabetes. I remained in ICU for two weeks. My pain in my head was so bad that when my heart would beat, my head would feel pain. I had just begun my masters of arts in urban ministry at Trinity International Divinity School in Deerfield, Illinois. I asked the Lord what he wanted me to do. He responded, "Finish what you started." The medical treatment I received stopped the bleeding. The insulin got the diabetes under control.

In 2015, the tumor returned. This time, four times larger than 2006. I was informed by my neurologist that if non-abrasive laser treatment does not work, I would have to have my nose removed. They would have to remove my nose to get to the base of my skull. Because of Obamacare, the procedure was covered by Medicaid. I had five treatments which lasted for twenty minutes each. The tumor was reduced to less than the size of a dime. Unfortunately, there is no guarantee that the tumor will not return. If I had known what faith means, I learned that when I was too sick to pray and when I could not communicate to my doctors about what was going on, I realized that only God knew. Only God could relay the message. My faith grew from faith to faith.

CHAPTER 2

Practical Word of God

The Practical Word of God is based on four theories:

- Practicing the Word of God
- Profit of the Word of God
- Purpose of the Word of God
- Possible through the Word of God

A. Practicing the Word of God

> "That which was from the beginning, which we have heard, which we have seen with our eyes, which we have looked upon, and our hands have handled of the Word of Life" (1 John 1:1, KJV).

Being practical suggests that we present the Word of God not as a theory, speculation, or ideal but as the inspired Word of God which we have acquired through practice or action.

In the Epistle, John wrote to prove (Christ's) humanity, assuming his (Christ's) deity throughout. This emphasis shows that early Gnosticism was a problem to the believers and that they needed instruction. Gnosticism considered matter as evil; and thus, Christ could not have a human body. Their Docetism (which taught that Christ only appeared or seemed to have a body) had to be confronted.

"…which was from the beginning…"

> "In the beginning was the Word, and the Word
> was with God, and the Word was God. The
> same was in the beginning with God…And
> the Word was made flesh and dwelt among us"
> (John 1:1–2;14, KJV).

Who has been from the beginning? Jesus. When God said "Let us make man" in Genesis 1:26, he was talking to Jesus and the Holy Spirit (the Godhead or Trinity).

"…which we have heard…"

> "So then faith cometh by hearing and hearing by
> the Word of God" (Romans 10:17, KJV).

> "How then shall they call on him whom they have
> not believed? And how shall they believe in him
> of whom they have not heard? And how shall they
> hear without a preacher" (Romans 10:14, KJV)?

What have we heard from the beginning?

> "Behold I was shaped in iniquity; and in sin did
> my mother conceive me" (Psalm 51:5, KJV).

We have blamed the Scripture for the condition of sin that is in our lives. Scriptures are not to be blamed for our sins, for the Scriptures also state, "For all have sinned, and come short of the Glory of God" (Romans 3:23, KJV).

Have you heard how you can be saved from all of your sins?

> That if you shalt confess with thy mouth the
> Lord Jesus, and shalt believe in thine heart that

God hath raised him from the dead, then thou shalt be saved. (Romans 10:9, KJV).

And the things that thou hast heard of me among many witnesses, the same commit thou to faithful men, who shall be able to teach others also. (2 Timothy 2:2, KJV)

Which we have seen with our eyes...

Jesus saith unto him, "Thomas, because thou hast seen me, thou hast believed: blessed are they that have not seen, and yet have believed." (John 20:29, KJV)

No, I was not at the foot of the cross like John. I was not at Calvary when they crucified my Jesus. I was not there when they pierced him in the side when blood and water came gushing out. I was not there when he gave up the Ghost. I was not there when he was laid in a borrowed tomb, and neither was I there on the third day when he rose from the grave—having all power in heaven and earth in his hand. I was not there when doubting Thomas saw for himself the nail prints in his hands and the wound in his side, which was inflicted at Calvary's cross. No! I was not there that day! But when I look into the spirit realm, I can visualize Calvary. I can see my Jesus "...wounded for our (my) transgressions, he was bruised for our (my) iniquities the chastisement of our (my) peace was upon him; and with his stripe we (I) am healed" (Isaiah 53:5, KJV).

No, I was not there, "But my spirit beareth witness with His Spirit that Jesus laid down his life for me and took it up again for me that I might have a right to the Tree of Life" (Revelations 22:14).

But blessed are your eyes, for they see: and your ears, for they hear. For verily I say unto you that many prophets and righteous men have desired to see those things which ye see, and have not seen

them: and hear those things which ye hear, and
have not heard them. (Matthew 13:16–17, KJV)

Then Jesus answering said unto them, "Go your
way, and tell John what things ye have seen and
heard; how that the blind see, the lame walk, the
lepers are cleansed, the deaf hear and the dead are
raised, to the poor the gospel is preached. And
blessed is he, whosoever shall not be offended in
me." (Luke 7:22–23, KJV)

When we consider the practical application of the Word of
God, we must consider what can be practiced and what is profitable,
purposeful, and possible.

"The husband that laboureth must be first partaker of the fruits" (2 Timothy 2:6, KJV).

This verse of Scripture proclaims that before anyone can lead
someone to Christ, they must first go themselves. Before we can help
someone get to know Jesus in the power of his resurrection and the
fellowship of his suffering, we must first experience it. Then we will
possess the fruits or the visible expression of power working inwardly
and invisibly, the character of the fruit being evidence of the character of the power producing it.

The husbandman refers to a tiller of ground or a witness for
Jesus. And this witness had to labor or grow weary in deliverance and
experience what it is like to go through withdrawals or drying out with
the stench of nicotine coming out of their pores along with other personal battles. This witness first had to be a partaker. In other words, go
through the process of deliverance before others can be led through.

After trying to live the American dream, I made a commitment
to live a Christian life without the worldly desires of materialism. I
made a quality decision in 1989 to try the Lord. Not only did I want
to see if he (the Lord) was real, but I wanted to test every word in the
Bible that pertained to a born-again believer.

> "Trust in the Lord with all thine heart and lean not unto thine own understanding. In all thy ways acknowledge him, and he shall direct thy paths" (Proverbs 3:5–6, KJV).

This was my memory verse that enabled me to begin to trust solely in Jesus and his delivering power. Unto this day, I have never been forsaken nor have I had to beg for bread in order to instruct on how God is able to heal, deliver, and set the captives free; it was my lot to experience drug addiction, alcoholism, depression, and poverty. My conviction is that we are anointed in the area of our lives that God has prepared us and brought us through. We are only as great as our greatest conviction.

Being filled with the Spirit of God, sanctified (separated and set aside for God's service) and purged by the blood of Jesus for spiritual advancement, I can look back on the Word of God that I practiced on a daily basis which enabled me to be considered by God as fit for the Master's use.

At the age of twenty-nine, I found myself addicted to cocaine or rocks. This bondage to the Spirit of Apollyon (the destroyer and keeper to the bottomless pit (Revelations 9:11) was brought on by a state of depression. One night, I recalled that I purchased $100 worth of cocaine or rocks. During that time, I could get up to ten rocks for that amount of money. I owned a townhouse in Las Vegas, Nevada. My wife left me the townhouse as part of a divorce settlement. I went upstairs and sat in a dark walk-in closet. I closed the door and was only using a torch made with Everclear and cotton balls as light. I smoked all ten rocks one after another. As far as I was concerned, I was trying to commit suicide, but God had his hands on me! God knew that he had anointed and preordained me to preach his gospel from the foundations of the world. So to this day, I am persuaded that my life is not my own.

> What shall we say then? Shall we continue in sin, that grace may abound? God forbid. How shall we, that are dead to sin, live any longer

therein? Know ye not, that so many of us as were baptized in Jesus Christ were baptized into his death? Therefore we are buried with him by baptism into death: that like as Christ was raised up from the dead by the glory of the Father, even so we also should walk in newness of life. (Romans 6:1–4, KJV)

"I am crucified with Christ: nevertheless I live; yet not I, but Christ liveth in me: and the life which I now live in the flesh I live by the faith of the Son of God, who loved me, and gave himself for me" (Galatians 2:20, KJV).

Reconciliation began for me one Monday morning in November, 1989. I had just returned to my barracks while serving in the Armed Forces. I had been out partying, which I had done as often as I could. Someone had placed a note on my door from my nephew back home. The note read: Call home. Danny is dead.

Danny was my closest brother. A brother that I had never argued with and one I had always been able to communicate with. I called home, and my mother told me he died of an apparent heart attack. Dead at the age of thirty-eight because of his continuous bondage to alcohol. I knew from past conversations that Danny was not saved.

Immediately, I began to blame myself for not accepting my calling to preach the gospel (ten years earlier) as the reason why Danny was not saved. In the midst of self-condemnation, I fell to my knees and begged God to give me another chance; and if he would, I would live for him. Rivers of tears of repentance began to flow from my eyes. Never had I cried like that in my life—not knowing if tears would ever stop. Then just like that, as if God had turned the faucet on, he turned it off. The tears dried up. I believe that God looks at our tears under a microscope to check their sincerity. At that very moment, I found peace with God that passes all understanding. It was years later that I found out that Danny had been baptized at an early age. His passing was my wake-up call.

FRANKLIN L. ELMORE

Still having vices to deal with, I began reading the Word of God.
I found in the Gospel of Matthew 6:13 which says, "And lead us not
into temptation, but deliver us from evil." A verse of the Scripture
was where Jesus was teaching his disciples the manner by which they
should pray. On a daily basis, I was able to practice this Scripture. I
believe this Scripture was telling me, "Lord, if you don't lead me to
the rock house, I won't go either." So until the craving for cocaine
had subsided, I meditated on Matthew 6:13.

Another struggle I had was with alcohol. When the craving
for rocks (cocaine) would become too strong, I would drink until
I become intoxicated. Too intoxicated to go and buy more drugs.
Often, I would drink until I passed out as an assurance that I could
not go to the drug dealer. One day, I was invited to church by a
coworker. The choir sang a song called "Jesus Is the Rock of My
Salvation." I asked Jesus to take away the craving for cocaine and
deliver me from the Spirit of Apollyon; and as if he had been waiting
on me to ask, he delivered me immediately.

The craving stopped. However, I still had a drinking problem. I
was able to drink socially. I did not have to drown out the craving for
drugs. For the next two years, the Holy Spirit (which convicts us of
sin, judgment, and righteousness) began convicting me of drinking,
smoking cigarettes, cursing, and fornication. It took a total of three
years for deliverance, but God delivered me out of them all. Today I
can tell you that I am free from those bondages. I am a spirit-filled
born-again (regenerated from above) believer. In three years, God
purged me from the sins that so easily beset me. Yes, he did it just
like that.

As time passed, I had a dream that I was trying to join a church
choir. I was auditioning with two women, and only one of us would
be selected. The chorus line of the song was "Let them spark, let
there be spades." In my dream, I was a pretty good singer. But I was
not good enough to be part of the choir. One of the other women
was selected. God had a rhema word for me. I believe God was speaking to me saying, "Let the people that have been preaching for many
years that have not understood the mystery or knowledge of Christ
continue. They have been like John the Baptist, turning souls to

Christ. But you will not only turn souls to Christ as a spade. I will use you to plant a seed of hope, life, purpose, prosperity, and the practical significance of being a child of God."

"Verily, verily, I say unto you. Except a corn of wheat fall into the ground and die, it abided alone: but if it die, it bringeth forth much fruit" (John 12:24, KJV).

"But be ye doers of the Word, and not hearers only, deceiving your own selves" (James 1:22, KJV).

Many people have joined a church and attended services faithfully only to become a pew member. They are overly cautious about stepping out on faith. They listen to a messenger but will not apply the message to their lives. One reason for their failure to receive a *rhema* (the individual Scripture which the Spirit brings to our remembrance for use in time of need) word from God is self-righteousness.

All the ways of a man are clean in his own eyes but the Lord weigheth the Spirit. (Proverbs 16:2, KJV)

What I tell you in darkness, that speak ye in light: and ye hear in the ear, that preach ye upon the house top. (Matthew 10:27, KJV)

All that I proclaim is a direct result of the information and revelation I have received from the Holy Spirit. Practical Word Ministries is not my brainchild. It is the charge that I have received as a platform to reach the multitude that does not have a relationship with God.

According to the glorious gospel of the blessed God, which was committed to my trust. And I thank Christ Jesus our Lord, who hath enabled me, for he counted me faithful, putting me into the ministry. (1 Timothy 1:11–12, KJV).

> Study to shew thyself approved unto God, a work-
> man that needeth not be ashamed rightly divid-
> ing the Word of Truth. (2 Timothy 2:15, KJV)

The desire of every ministry proceeding from God should be to be approved or endorsed by God (anointed). Yet in today's society, ministries are more interested in recognition from a multimillion dollar ministry than from God, the source of all that they desire to accomplish. Jesus was an itinerate preacher preaching to the multitudes and then only to a few. We should follow his example of preaching the gospel to the poor—those who cannot afford to pay $1,000 or a thirty-minute summation.

> Ever learning and never able to come to the
> knowledge of the truth. (2 Timothy 3:7, KJV)

> For we walk by faith, not by sight. (2 Corinthians
> 5:7, KJV)

The more we operate or exercise our faith, the more we will walk by faith and not by sight. I will continue to allow the Lord to order my footsteps. In those steps, I will find something of value to share.

B. Profit of the Word of God

> "Now, brethren, if I come unto you speaking
> with tongues, what shall I profit you, except I
> shall speak to you either by revelation or by
> knowledge, or by prophesying, or by doctrine"
> (1 Corinthians 14:6, KJV).

The Word of God should be capable of being used or put into effect. The Apostle Paul was explaining to the Church in Corinth that it will profit them more if he spoke to them in a language they could understand. Communication is the transmission and reception of thought on a level common to both the sender and receiver. During that period of the apostle's ministry, the Church in Corinth would have an entire meeting when all the members would speak in tongues. Can you picture visiting a church and for three hours, everyone is speaking in an unknown tongue? This particular event is a reminder of my first encounter with the Catholic Church service. I went to the service ignorant of their doctrine and traditions. The parishioners began to speak Latin of which I did not understand. Therefore, I did not receive anything from God. I left the service, still desiring reconciliation with God.

People have asked me why they have not been able to speak in tongues. The Bible states that tongues are evidence of the indwelling of the Holy Spirit. So people may say, "I know I am filled with the Holy Spirit but I still cannot speak in tongues." Let me assure you that if you have not spoken fluently in tongues, it is because you have not exercised that gift. Tongues are a gift from God which is given by grace to mature believers.

How do I know if I am a mature believer? When you understand the purpose of the gifts of the Spirit. Tongues are given for four reasons:

1. Edifying of self.
2. Edifying of church.
3. Make intercession for the body of Christ.
4. Make intercession for the will of God in earth.

Now that you know what tongues are for and you desire to accomplish on of its purposes, then ask the Holy Spirit, and he will not withhold any good thing from you.

> What do it profit, my brethren, though a man may say he hath Faith, and have not works? Can faith save him? If a brother or sister be naked, and destitute of daily food, and one of you say unto them, Depart in peace, be ye warmed and filled; notwith-

standing ye give them not those things which are needful to the body; what doeth it profit? Even so Faith if it hath not works, is dead being alone. Yea, a man say, Thou hath faith, and I have works: shew me thy faith without thy works, and I will show thee my faith by my works. (James 2:14–18, KJV)

James is simply saying that words without action produces little. If we show no love, then are we really producing the fruits of righteousness? The Bible says,

Faith without works is dead, yet taking it a little further, works without love is dead. (James 2:17)

And how I kept back nothing that was profitable unto you, but shewed you, and have taught you publicly, and from house to house. (Acts 20:20, KJV)

Because of my previous reputation, a preacher told me not to tell everything God had done for me. In other words, keep my testimony in the closet. However, "I am crucified with Christ: nevertheless I live; yet not I, but Christ liveth in me: and the life which I now live in the flesh I live by the faith of the Son of God, who loved me, and gave himself for me" (Galatians 2:20, KJV).

I have no reputation to uphold other than living holy as an ambassador for Christ. I believe God healed, delivered, and set me free from my bondage of sin. Now my life can be a living testimony to his saving power. To suppress that testimony is to be ashamed of the blessedness of God. If God has delivered you from addictions, don't worry about what man will say. Man's finite mind cannot perceive the wonder working power of our own testimony. It has been said, and I agree that it is hard for a crackhead to believe the report of deliverance from someone who has never been dependent on the drug themselves. As with pastors, some will only believe what another pastor interprets to be true concerning the Word of God and doctrines of that particular denomination.

Likewise, ye younger, submit yourselves unto the elder, Yea, all of you be subject to one another, and be clothed with humility: For God resisteth the proud, and giveth grace to the humble. (1 Peter 5:5, KJV)

All scripture is given by inspiration of God, and is profitable for doctrine, for reproof, for correction, for instruction in righteousness: That the man of God may be perfect, thoroughly furnished unto all good works. (2 Timothy 3:16–17, KJV)

Whereof I was made a minister, according to the gift of the grace of God given unto me by the effectual working of his power [Holy Spirit]. Unto me, who am less than the least of all saints, is this grace given; that I should preach among the Gentiles the unsearchable riches of Christ; and to make all men see what is the fellowship of the mystery, which from the beginning of the world hath hidden in God, who created all things by Jesus Christ: To the intent that now unto the principalities and powers in heavenly places might be known by the Church the manifold wisdom of God, according to the eternal purpose which he purposed in Christ Jesus our Lord; In whom we have boldness and access with confidence by the Faith of him [Jesus]. (Ephesians 3:7–12, KJV)

C. Purpose of the Word of God

The Word of God is designed to serve a purpose without elaboration. Too many times, graduates of seminaries, I mean, seminaries have spoken eloquently yet have not reach the people. They have not challenged the congregation of the saints to understand and fulfill

God's purposes for their lives. God's Word is a simple message. A child understands the way of salvation.

> "That if thou shalt confess with thy mouth the Lord Jesus and shalt believe in thine heart that God hath raised him from the dead, thou shalt be saved" (Romans 10:9, KJV).

The Word of God carries the purpose of the church which is to destroy the works of the devil. It also carries the purpose of mankind which is to give God all the praise and all the glory.

> "Every purpose is established by counsel: and with good advice make war" (Proverbs 20:18, KJV).

The Bible tells us to wait on our ministry. The reason we should wait is because God is trying to convey a message to us. Wait until we hear with our spiritual ear, not when man says *go*.

> "And we know that all things work together for the good to them that love God, to them who are the called according to hi purpose" (Romans 8:28, KJV).

We should never forget who calls and who purposes. If we forget who calls, then who are we following? If we forget who purposes, then who are we serving? Practical Word Ministries commission aims to help believers begin to understand their calling and act upon that understanding.

> "Wherefore rather, brethren, give diligence to make your calling and election sure: for if ye do these things, ye shall never fall: For so an entrance shall be ministered unto you abundantly into the everlasting kingdom of our Lord and Saviour Jesus Christ" (2 Peter 1:10–11, KJV).

D. *Possible through the Word of God*

> "Jesus saith unto him, 'If thou canst believe,
> all things are possible to him that believeth'"
> (Mark 9:23, KJV).

The Word of God was written so that man would know that which is impossible with man is possible with God.

> "But Jesus beheld them, and saith unto them,
> 'With men this is impossible; but with God all
> things are possible'" (Matthew 19:26, KJV).

There may be something in your life that seems like it's impossible to handle. Maybe your marriage has been torn so far apart that it does not seem as if it can be repaired. You are ready to get a divorce on the grounds of irreconcilable differences. Maybe you have full blown AIDS, and you are about to curse God and die. Or maybe your children have shattered all the plans you have made for their lives. Or maybe you are like who I used to be—without hope, merely existing, searching for death as a haven. Could it be you are homeless, going from shelter to shelter or even contemplating suicide? Ask yourself this question, *Is anything too hard for God?*

> But we have this treasure in earthen vessels, that
> the excellency of the power may be of God,
> and not of us. We are troubled on every side,
> yet not distressed; we are perplexed, but not in
> despair; Persecuted, but not forsaken; cast down,
> but not destroyed; always bearing about in the
> body the dying of the Lord Jesus, that the life
> also of Jesus might be manifest in our body.
> (2 Corinthians 4:7–10, KJV)

CHAPTER 3

New Member's Class

The purpose of *My PFP* is to equip new Christians with the information required to become functional members of a local church. It is the pastor's responsibility to ensure that every member's introduction into their ministry is a smooth transition. Postmodernism and other cultural traditions bring additional problems to preparing new members for service in a local church. The pastor should gain the wisdom and expertise to guide the teachers and new members in understanding the *practical foundational principles* in a local church.

Take the time and provide new members with the information necessary for them to become functional members of the local church. Each new member will have voting rights as all other members. Therefore, it is imperative that they understand godly principles that govern the church. Upon receiving the right hand of fellowship, they have all rights and privileges as any other member. It is incumbent upon the pastor to ensure each new member is cognitive of those rights and privileges. A new member's class will provide an atmosphere of illumination and reflection on the intricacies of the church.

It will also begin the process of teaching spiritual growth across the lifespan of a disciple of Jesus Christ. The church has a responsibility to explain and teach every aspect of who God is to a believer. Through such nurturing, a relationship will be born between the believer and God. The church is designed by God to build relationships not only with him but also with one another.

My PFP shall depict Christian education as a system that brings life. It speaks to eradicating the devils hold on the lives of disciples. Christian education takes the mission of Christ and fulfills that mission in the life of the church. Therefore, the church needs to be a demonstration of Christ.

A. Living Organism

The attitude of disciples regarding Christian education must be renewed in the spirit of their minds. The church is not a gathering place for the rich and famous nor does it exist to do church work, but it is a living organism—an organism that gives life to God's children. After reviewing this model of Christian education, a church should implement or improve on the mission of making disciples become like Christ. The following topics will be discussed: centrality of the Word of God, thinking process, the development process, and God's involvement in this process. First let's look at the centrality of the Word of God.

B. Centrality of the Word of God

The centrality of the Word of God is necessary for the spiritual maturity of a disciple across their lifespan. As a child, the Bible says we know the way of salvation through the gospel. If this is so, we must teach children to understand who God is. We must not make God out to be simply love and merciful. We must also show God to be just and to be feared.

There are two detrimental results of not having a proper fear of God. First sin will more easily abound without the fear of God to restrain it. Second not fearing God reduces our appreciation of God's mercy.[1]

Spiritual maturity begins with knowledge of the Bible. A Christian educator should teach the sixty-six books of the Bible as a love story between God and man. The Word of God must be taught in relation to real life, not as academic information detached from the experiences of people. The Word of God must be taught as truth to be lived, not simply as knowledge to be understood.

The practice of altering Scripture has no advantage in growing faith kids. Faith kids are those who respond to a faith relationship with God through Jesus Christ and continue to grow in that relationship.[2]

Christian education may alter the method of teaching but never alter the message. The Bible is not to be mistrusted; we must teach it as the inspired Word of God. Jesus proclaimed that he did not come to change the Word of God but to fulfill it. Christians must learn that the Word of God is the only rule of faith. The Bible proclaims that "faith cometh by hearing and hearing by the Word of God."

Now let's discuss the thinking process of disciples across their lifespan.

C. Thinking Process

Because God has spoken and his Word is truth, spiritual maturity involves how we think.[3]

New member's class should understand that people do not think and learn the same way. Christians should recognize that wisdom is the proper application of knowledge.

Babes in Christ————Others Feel————Spiritually Mature

Three Levels of Decision-Making

There are three levels of decision-making methods used by Christians. First there are the babes in Christ that make their decisions based on how they feel about the Word of God and how it relates to their way of life. Second there are Christians who are influenced in their decision-making by the way others feel and the rules that govern them. Thirdly there are spiritually mature Christians that consider how God feels.

These three methods of decision-making will affect not only the individual lives of Christians but also how they serve God. A spiritually mature Christian will give and serve according to how God feels not according to doctrinal rules. Colossians 2:2 says we should love God with our minds. As new member class instructors, we have the responsibility of having the minds of believers renewed by the Word of God. When disciples begin to love God with their minds, their approach to a right relationship with him will be according to his Word. The mind helps determine how we process the knowledge of God. Whether disciples are dealing with issues of God's grace or mercy, how they react to life and the church will be based on their understanding of the relationship they have with God.

So the *Practical Foundational Principles* should contain instructions regarding the different levels of Christian decision-making and faith based on the Word of God. If a new member's class is to be affective, it must recapture a proper understanding of the role of the mind in spiritual growth.[4]

So let's look at how the developmental process is essential to spiritual growth.

D. Developmental Process

The *Practical Foundational Principles* is the teaching of the whole person. The centrality of the new member's class begins with addressing the whole body. The New Testament stresses that as believers, we should love God with all of our heart, mind, soul, and might. The new member's class in this church should consider how the developmental process impacts the discipleship of its members across their lifespan.

The new member's class should follow the model used by Jesus called *triangle effect*. The triangle effect involves teaching the head, heart, and hands. Hebrews 4 explains how the head is where cognitive thinking exists. The heart is where relational feeling and how one believes. The hands represent application on an individual's own volition. The triangle effect addresses the Christian state, position, and arrival point. When God gets into a believer's life, it affects the way they act, think, and feel. The first process in developing mature Christians is establishing a relationship with Christ to know God. When a new member joins the church, they should have progressive steps toward growing into the image of Christ. These steps should include foundation classes, Christian development classes, and leadership classes. These steps should help produce spiritually mature Christians.

Deuteronomy 6:4–9 discusses *shema* which is a pattern of instruction that focuses on the responsibility of the parent to impress God's commands upon their children.[5]

The Bible says, "Train up a child in the way they should go, and when they are old, they will not depart from it." The new member's class should consider having parents become instrumental in the spiritual development of their children. After looking at the developmental process, it's time to consider God's involvement in the process of teaching for spiritual growth.

The question was raised, "Can faith development be taught?" The answer is *no*, not without God's intervention. The Bible says faith is a gift from God. So faith without God's intervention will not develop discipleship across the lifespan of a believer. The Practical Foundational Principles class should teach that God has to be involved in the lives of disciples across their lifespan. God can do what we cannot. It is our responsibility as educators to get a disciple's attention regarding their relationship with God. But God will be the one who gets their lives.

Faith is not something to create in people. Faith is a gift from God. The number one priority is that God will touch their hearts and give them faith. Faith is an action word. When people profess to have faith, they are professing to a way of life. A way of life that says, "I will trust God with all my heart and lean not to my own understanding." However, there are some Christians who feel that healing, deliverance, and sanctification can be accomplished on their own volition. Christians sometimes say they know the will of God for their lives. Just because a person knows the will of God for their life does not mean they will do it. The power must come from God to accomplish his will in the life of a believer.

E. God's Involvement

God's purpose for the church is modeling fellowship with him. As a young man in the early '70s, I can recall my first encounter with the Holy Spirit. I was singing in a choir at Mt. Moriah Missionary Baptist Church in Paducah, Kentucky. The church was in the process of building a new facility. We were meeting in the community center on the South Side of Paducah. While singing, I felt something come over me that had never happened before. As I sang, tears began flowing from my eyes. I sat down for fear of shame. God forbid. Someone saw me and said that I was too sentimental as a man. I had never heard of such an emotion for a man. I never told anyone about it. I know now that God was trying to tell me something. Through the Holy Spirit, God was trying to establish a relationship with me. The Practical Foundational Principles class should have a curriculum that deals with real issues without which, it will be talking about theory.

In keeping the centrality of the Word of God and not allowing personal experiences to dictate the truth of the Bible, it is possible to deal with real issues in a theological manner. The Father will ultimately decide the relationship God wants to have with a disciple. For only the Father can bring his children to maturity. God allows us graciously to teach his children using thinking and developmental processes, but we could never produce the fruits of righteousness in another person by our own will and effort.

Spiritual maturity involves the whole person. Maturity has to do with how we think, where we place our affections, and how we behave. It is cognitive, affective, and volitional involving mind, heart, and will. It requires a complete educational perspective.[6]

All of these should be considered in our Practical Foundational Principles class.

Christian Journey

The PFP class will show the viability and worth it has to the student. The PFP are the principles of God that will enable each new member to begin their Christian journey with a zeal of God according to knowledge.

Introduction————Hermeneutics————Mission/Vision

Three Focuses of PFP

There are three major focuses of the Practical Foundational Principles: 1) introduction to the ministry; 2) biblical hermeneutics; and 3) mission and vision of the church. The introduction of the ministry will include the history of the church. The biblical hermeneutics will address each new members understanding of biblical principles. As Southern Baptist, the constitution, bylaws, and decrees differ from postmodern religions. The mission and vision of the church will discuss both a living statement and where the new members believe they should serve.

The Practical Foundational Principles will last for twelve weeks. Twelve weeks will be long enough to cover the required materials. During this time, the new members will be given the opportunity to volunteer with additional outreach and hospitality programs. The classes will be one hour in length. They will follow morning worship services. The time is very convenient for all who are involved. The class will be located in the fellowship hall of the church.

The instructors will include the pastor, associate ministers, or other laypersons of the church. The associate ministers and laypersons will take part of the first new member's class. They will also be trained in dealing with the different cultures, denominations, and postmodern thinking of the new members. They will also be prepared to answer questions regarding the faith and direction of the church. It will be understood that the pastor can be called to clarify any major conflicts in discussions. The target audiences are from twelve to eighty years of age. Children normally attend with their parents and guardians. They will eventually have their own new member's class. At this time, adolescents and adults are old enough to be baptized and understand the relevancy of Scripture. The church's average age is thirty. Some new members will come from Catholic,

Muslim, Jehovah's Witness, Holiness, and Seventh-Day Adventist backgrounds. It will be a cross-cultural mixture of Hispanic, African-American, Anglo Saxon, European, and Asian people. The cross-cultural congregation will be prepared to worship and serve God in a Christian culture.

Each new member will benefit from the project. Their understanding of the biblical principles of God and decrees of the church will enable them to become functional members of the church. There are no insignificant members in the body of Christ. Therefore, the church must equip each new member with the tools to become affective in their calling.

CHAPTER 4

Introduction of Ministry

In 1987, I received my calling to be a servant of the Lord. Since that time, my life has changed dramatically. I called it a significant emotional journey of faith. I have gone from the depths of sin to the grace of God. I was ordained a gospel minister in 1998. I began my formal education at Trinity International University–Chicago campus in 2001. I received a BA in Christian ministry in the Reach program in 2005. I have been pastoring for sixteen years. The growth of our church membership makes it necessary to create an effective new member's class. A class that will enable new converts and those recommitting their lives to Christ to become functional members of the body of Christ. Paul wrote that he would not have the church ignorant concerning spiritual things. The Word of God persuades me that Christians are children of light. Therefore, they should not be in darkness concerning the ways and principles of God.

My PFP class enabled me to use the tools I have received during the ten years of my formal education. The development and training of other teachers will help me grow spiritually and become more humble. The education of other Christian journeymen is a calling I have accepted from the Lord. This class will allow me the opportunity to prepare the way for future Christian education. Our ministry is to enable men to take their proper places in the body of Christ. It is to prepare the daughters of Zion for their exalted roles in the body of Christ. And finally, to mentor our youth in the nurture and admonition of the Lord.

A. Biblical Hermeneutics

My PFP is both biblical and theological. New members are those who come by Christian experience (because they are coming from another Baptist churches and cannot receive a letter from that church); those coming from another denomination that have not been immersed in water will be baptized; those who restore their membership (they were members but were inactive for a period of time); and new converts to the Christian faith.

Perry G. Downs declared that learning is not the enemy of freedom; and doing is not the enemy of discovery. "If people are to act like Christians, they must think like Christians. If people are to think like Christians, they must first know what Scripture says and what it require of them."[7]

> [W]hen all Israel comes to appear before the Lord your God at the place which He will choose, you shall read this law in front of all Israel in their hearing: "Assemble the people, the men and the women and children and the alien who is in your town, so that they may hear and learn and fear the Lord your God, and be careful to observe all the words of this law." (Deuteronomy 31:11b–12, NASB)

Moses instructed all of Israel to learn and remember the sovereignty of God.

> Now we have received, not the spirit of the world, but the Spirit who is from God, so that we may know the things freely given to us by God, which things we also speak, not in words taught by human wisdom, but those taught by the Spirit, combining spiritual thoughts with spiritual words. (1 Corinthians 2:12–13, NASB)

The Holy Spirit is responsible for revealing the truth of God's Word to all that call upon him. The disciples of Jesus did not understand the words of Jesus until after the Holy Ghost fell on them in Acts 2. A new convert may not receive the truth of the Word of God until after the Holy Spirit reveals it to them.

"Be diligent to present yourself approved to God as a workman who does not need to be ashamed, accurately handling the word of truth" (2 Timothy 2:15, NASB). The Practical Foundational Principles class will direct a new convert's zeal in the right direction. Some have a zeal of God but not according to knowledge. The new member's class will help new members focus on the practical application of the Word of God.

> Therefore I urge you, brethren, by the mercies of God, to present your bodies a living and holy sacrifice, acceptable to God, which is your spiritual service of worship. And do not be conformed to this world, but be transformed by the renewing of your mind, so that you may prove what the will of God is, that which is good and acceptable and perfect. (Romans 12:1–2, NASB)

A Christian is to come before the Lord as a yielded vessel. They must realize that their bodies have become the temple of the living God. They are no longer in bondage to the lust of the eye, flesh, or pride of life. The vain imaginations and traditions of man will no longer control a new member's cognitive thinking. The Holy Spirit will begin a regenerative work that will cause both the conscious and subconscious minds to focus on the holiness and wisdom of God. Because our will is not our own, the PFP will direct a new member back to the will of God for their lives. They will be instructed that in the will of God are the provisions of life.

"He who has my commandments and keeps them is the one who loves me; and he who loves me will be loved by my Father, and I will love him and will disclose myself to him" (John 14:21, NASB).

The PFP will reveal the ways God has showed his love for them. It will also discuss the general and natural revelation concepts.[8]

> Go therefore and make disciples of all the nations, baptizing them in the name of the Father and the Son and the Holy Spirit, teaching them to observe all that I commanded you; and lo, I am with you always, even to the end of the age. (Matthew 28:19–20, NASB)

Jesus instructed his disciples to share the gospel message. He wanted them to continue the ordinance of water baptism. He also wanted his disciples to know that he would never leave them alone. A new member's class should teach the obedience to the ordinances in Scripture.

The scope and limitations of the PFP class is to reveal the curriculum of the Practical Foundational Principles class. The following topics will discussed: 1) history of church; 2) ministries; 3) affiliations; and 4) mission statement.

B. History of Church

The ministry was chartered in October of 1998 by Franklin L. Elmore as the Practical Word Ministries. It began at a teenage mothers' group home on the Southside of Chicago. There were weekly Bible study and prayer meetings with foster care teenage girls that had children out of wedlock. The ministry then moved to 1152 Summer St. in Hammond Indiana in 2003. The membership rose to thirty. During this time, more than fifteen people were baptized. There was Wednesday Bible study and prayer meeting. The outreach ministry began by giving hot meals to residents of Harvey, Illinois.

By 2005, the members decided to rent their first worship center at 5928 Willis Ave. in Hammond, Indianna. We began having Sunday school and morning worship services. The new membership grew to over forty. There were three deacons ordained. The ministry continued its outreach in Harvey, Illinois.

C. Ministry of Church

In 2007, the ministry moved back to Chicago at 9521 S. LaSalle. The basement of the pastor was remodeled into a fellowship hall. The church purchased chairs, tables, and pulpit furniture. An organ was donated. The Friendship Corner outreach ministry began distributing tons of food and clothing monthly. We continued to minister in Harvey, Illinois. The church began having afternoon services and other outings. The membership grew to over fifty by 2009. The church licensed its first associate female minister in 2009. It also began a theology class every Wednesday evening. The church continued to minister to the community with biannual fish fries. The fish fries were served over seventy-five people to transit, homeless, and low income in the Roseland community.

Practical Word Ministries has a weekly theology class every Wednesday at 7:00 p.m. The theology class is a pre-college course for licensed ministers and those seeking a better understanding of Scripture. The goal of the class is to prepare its students to seek a formal education. We realize that a formal education such as Trinity International Universities Reach Program will equip the students with the tools they will need to interpret Scripture for their lifespan.

There is an outreach ministry called the Friendship Corner. Working with local and state agencies, the outreach ministry donates food, clothing, and hot meals to the homeless and low income in our community. Over ten tons of food and clothing are distributed on an annual basis. Sunday morning, Bible studies began at 12:00 p.m. During this time, the members were disciples and were given an opportunity to participate in the learning process. We recognized that adults learn from one another; therefore, the Bible study is full of experience and illuminations from people of different cultures and backgrounds.

D. *Affiliations of Church*

Practical Word Ministries joined the Chicago Metropolitan Baptist Association in October of 2008. We joined the Illinois State Baptist Association in November of 2008. This affiliation gave us our 501c(3) status. In 2009, we received our Illinois Sales Tax Exempt letter.

We are affiliated with The Hands of Hope Ministry in Joliet Illinois. Through The Hands of Hope Ministry, we are able to get tons of food for distribution. We are also affiliated with the North American Missionary Board (NAMB) Southern Baptist which provided quarterly funding for our Hunger Ministries. The pastor is also a member of the Southern Baptist African American Pastor's Fellowship. They meet monthly to discuss issues common with African American pastors. They are also provided with conferences and workshops at no cost from the Southern Baptist Association.

E. *Mission Statement*

A mission statement identifies who your company is, what it does, what it stands for, and why you do it. It is a short statement that describes the company's story and ideals in less than thirty seconds.[9]

Practical Word Ministries Inc. is a non-profit organization sharing the gospel of Jesus Christ will all ethnic backgrounds—ministering to the spiritual and social needs of our community, nurturing the faith in our youth, and ministering on the principle that the practical application of the Word of God changes lives.[10]

The mission of sharing the gospel will be accomplished through evangelism, discipleship, and worship. We will be ministering to the spiritual and social needs in our community in spiritual counseling, administrative assistance, and outreach ministries. The youth will be nurtured in the faith as we teach for spiritual growth, mentoring, and community awareness.

The purpose of this information is to show the population with zip code 60628 on the South Side of the City of Chicago in

2008. The estimated population is 81,940 people. The population has decreased since 2000 by 6 percent from 87,827 according to City-Data.com. We will consider the fastest growing population and how our ministry would have to change to effectively minister. The following topics will be discussed: fastest growing population, evangelism, fellowship, discipleship, and worship. First let's begin with the fasting growing group in the 60628 zip code.

The fastest growing population is African American at 94 percent. The age group of five to ten-year-old children is the fastest growing among age groups. The church would have to make certain improvements to evangelism, fellowship, discipleship, and worship in order to minister to this age group.

The second faster growing population is Hispanic at 4.3 percent of the population. Throughout the City of Chicago, the Hispanic population has grown. Currently in the United States, there are over thirty-six million Hispanics. They have become the largest minority in the country.

The third fastest growing population is the white at 1 percent. The Roseland community, which is within the 60628 zip code, was 99 percent African American. Now Indo European people are moving into the area. The change is due to rising property values. Now let's look at how evangelizing to the youth would change in our ministry. Evangelism in the 60628 zip codes on the South Side of Chicago was where ten-year-old males are the fastest growing population. These are endangered species according to American Standards. They are targeted as the next generation of gang leaders, drug users, and convicts.

The church must reach out to these youth for Christ. Some of them are *unchurched*. Some are already involved in gangs. Some can be influenced to follow Christ. The church must institute an evangelistic ministry that will attract the youth instead of attacking their *known* culture.

Too many times, the church has offered a gospel message to the youth without considering their needs. When children live in dysfunctional families, it is imperative that youth leaders in the church live the life they are presenting. The evangelistic ministry would include activities that relate to the zeal of its youth. The youth should be exposed to every facet of life. A boy's ministry would seek to mentor the youth. Now let's consider how our fellowship would have to change.

F. Fellowship

In the City of Chicago one may see groups of young boys standing on street corners. Programs the government used to have are non-existent. Funding for after-school programs are now financing foreign wars. The church must work closely with its young black youth. Peer pressure is extreme at their age. The church must help them resist the temptation for the fast and glamorous appearance of life.

Academic training will serve as a buffer to a life of crime. The youth would be given additional assistance in their academic studies relating to reading, writing, mathematics, and science. Along with academics, career awareness would be offered. Youth with no options make choices based on ignorance.

Computer training would give the youth an advantage in education and life. The world of electronics and internet use has changed the way America and the world do business. It is very important for the youth to be computer literate. The church would obtain computers through various non-profit grants and organizations. Qualified instructors would give the training.

An after-school program would give the youth another avenue to avoid idleness at home and on the streets. It would allow for scriptural as well as secular deposits into their lives. Next let's look at how discipleship in the church would change.

Discipleship youth learn under different conditions than adults. The Sunday school department at our ministry would have to incorporate syllabus activities for youth. As a youth director, during my internship, I realized that youth learn more when they are actively involved. Lectures may not always capture their attention. They are stimulated to learn by hands-on activities.

Sunday school would separate the children based on awareness or age. The five-year-olds and twelve-year-olds retain information differently. It would be important to separate those groups in order to cut down on distractions. We would also have visual-aid teaching sessions. The youth of today have become used to watching TV, video games, and DVDs. They are a part of the new generation who depends on visual aids for instructions. The Sunday school would provide visual aids for instruction in biblical lessons. Finally let's consider how worship at our ministry would change to affect this population growth.

Worship ministry would have to prepare room for the youth to work in ministry. A children's church would allow the youth an opportunity to work in various ministries of the church.

When children work in the ministry, they have a sense of belonging. They would be allowed to serve during normal worship services as well. During these times, they would grow spiritually and intellectually. It would enhance their understanding of each worship service.

The children's church would prepare them for future ministry. The Bible encourages believers to train up a child in the way they should go; and when they are old, they would not depart from it. The children's church would make deposits that will last a lifetime.

The fastest growing population in the 60628 zip code is African American youth. Currently, males aged five to ten outnumber all other age groups. Our ministry would have to institute various programs such as evangelism toward youth, after-school fellowship programs, discipleship through Sunday school, and a children's church worship experience. These youth will become future church leaders. It is imperative that we instruct them early about the principles of God. They are our future educators and pastors. A strong religious background will help them fulfill their calling in life.

CHAPTER 5

Class Objectives

The first objective is to prepare new members with the foundational skills necessary to become functional members of the local church and body of Christ. Dysfunctional families and relationships are rampant in homes all over the country and state. The majority of children have grown up in a single-parent environment. The father is either in jail or on drugs. The mother has to be the father and disciplinarian. Or the mother is on drugs and has abandoned her children. There are abandoned children in DCFC. These children have conflicts as they grow older with their identity.

The Practical Foundational Principle class will seek to direct the new convert to their identity in Christ. The foundational skills will begin with the understanding and study of the creed of the local church. The creed represents what we, as a body of Christ, believe. According to Dr. Bruce L. Fields, the church is the means that God has ordained for the believer to give himself to the Lord and to fellow believers, and to obtain from them that, which is necessary for spiritual edification.[11]

The appendix attached will identify the creed of the church.[12]

Each new member will be required to sign a statement agreeing with the local church creed. The second objective is to identify specific groups in the local church that promotes a healthy church. There are six spiritual indicators of a healthy church. We will not attempt to discuss all six. We will focus on the holistic small group and the assimilation groups.[13]

The new member's class will have a holistic and fellowship group approach. At Trinity, Reach program taught the importance of small groups. It allows *hands-on* dialogue. There is time to consider the students' response to the Scripture. In a holistic small group, everyone can be realistic. In larger groups, it can be an impersonal environment. The holistic approach will seek to create a healthier church. Each member can receive individual attention. They will feel as important to the body of Christ as anyone else. Their witnessing will increase because of their personal experiences.

The assimilation fellowship group helps new members as well as visitors feel a part of the church, friendships, and address passions. The assimilation group will be used in our ministry. We want an atmosphere of family. Every eventual member should feel a part of an extended family. In every family, there are good and bad members. However, when there are personal crisis, even the bad members want to be involved. New members are given a membership list. The list does not include phone numbers, just address and names. They are encouraged to communicate with one another like families are supposed to do. We are not worried about internal divisions that would cause members to fall away from the ministry. We believe that God adds to the ministry daily such as should be saved.

The ministry encourages the establishment of friendships. Through working together in different areas of ministry, people establish interrelationships. Currently, every member at one time was a guest of another member. We believe that people may come to church services because a friend invited them. They do not come just because they liked the outside of the building or they heard the preaching/singing was so good. They come because they know someone who attends.

The third objective is to begin the process of fellowship and witnessing. God has not saved anyone to become a pew member. The class will help new members recognize their role in the body of Christ. Scripture tells a believer to make their calling and election sure. The class will aid the new members in recognizing their purpose and calling. The materials used to teach this class will come from Drukheim's book *Four Corners*. Discipleship creates an understanding of their identity in Christ. Accepting their calling reflects a response to that identity. Discipleship requires Christians to work together in order to reach the unity of the faith.

McRoberts writes in *Four Corners,* in Durkheim's opinion the, "Sacred and profane relied on each other for existence."[14]

In *Four Corners*, the street people posed different challenges for the churches. The churches perceived the streets as evil to be avoided, a recruitment ground or a point of contact for persons at risk. Chapter 5 focuses on the dominant religious interpretation of the street, street concepts, ambiguous roles that class and religious traditions played, and how taxonomy contributes to the ongoing urban social discussion. The new members will be cautioned on the absence of fellowship, the fear of witnessing and introduced to our local outreach ministry. These areas of ministry will help them prepare for discipleship. In *Four Corners*, the streets were full of so called evildoers. The congregation would not go door-to-door or remain after services for fellowship with one another.

The Reverend Robert Jameson, the pastor of Church of the Holy Ghost considered street people as *root workers.*[15]

He believed anyone from the street would be counter-productive for the church. Through behavior and worldly ways, root workers would destroy the fabric of the church. In turn, he felt the street people should come to him, not take the church to them.

The problem with the views of those who proclaim the streets as a place of evil to be avoided is fear. The fear becomes so real that fellowship with one another after services is avoided. The need to rush back to a safe environment after service reveals the absence of fellowship. Fellowship is one of the four essential elements of a functional church. The other elements are evangelism, discipleship, and worship. Without fellowship, the membership may become estranged to one another. A relationship without communication and fellowship with a foundation of fear lacks the potential for spiritual growth.

"Delivering thee from the people, and from the Gentiles, unto whom I send thee" (Acts 26:17, KJV). The Apostle Paul was given a divine mandate by God to go unto the people without fear of rejection. Christians should follow the example of Paul. The Bible also teaches that God has not given his children the spirit of fear. Yet many Christians refrain from witnessing about the gospel of Christ out of fear of the unknown. They do not know whom they will encounter. They are not sure what their reaction will be. Some are even afraid that they are not prepared to speak on behalf of God. Whatever the reason, the ability to proselytize those on the streets become hindered. Oftentimes, Christians forget what God had done in their lives. They forget that "for the grace of God goes us." Our expectation should not be laced with fear. We should believe there is no failure in God. A belief without fear should strengthen our faith in witnessing.

The new members would be introduced to the outreach ministry of your local church. The Friendship Corner is the outreach department of our church. At the Friendship Corner, mere handouts without responsibility will not be accepted. It is a place of assistance. Many people need another opportunity in life. Somehow, someway, they allowed the enemy to steal, kill, and destroy their lives. They are looking to take back everything the enemy has stolen or they allowed him to take.

The Friendship Corner offers the counseling and support for another opportunity in life. It helps put homeless people back into mainstream society. It reestablishes the relationships that were destroyed. The Friendship Corner tutors and mentors those who sincerely want a better lifestyle. As a faith-based ministry, it focuses on spiritual growth. For what would it profit a person to gain the whole world and still lose their soul?

A. Methodology

Practical Foundational Principles' new member's class should incorporate a certificate of new membership. You should devise a curriculum that will teach the principles of God's Word. The new member's classes would be held on a weekly basis for twelve weeks. The curriculum would be classes such as principles of salvation, disciples' prayer, faith development, covenant relationships, and preparing for urban ministry.[16]

Here are some examples of class methods:

The class on the principles of salvation will be in two sessions. The class will be one hour in duration. It will follow a morning worship service in the fellowship hall between 1:30 p.m. and 2:30 p.m. on Sundays. The new members will be required to complete this class prior to receiving their new member's certificate. The class will be offered three times per year. If the new member is unable to attend the class upon joining the church, they will have an opportunity to complete it the next time it is offered.

The class will be set up to accommodate twenty new members. There will be four sixteen-feet tables with five chairs at each table. The new members would be able to place their notebooks, Bibles, and other required materials on the table. The class would be designed to allow new members the personal space for laptop computers and other teaching aids.

The teacher would stand behind a podium during lectures. The podium will have a mic attached in order for the new members to hear clearly. Each new member will be required to have a Bible (KJV, NASB, or NIV). They will also need a notebook. They will be asked to read Scriptures and reflect on the Scriptures in relevance to their new Christian journey. The new member will receive a handout describing the lesson plan. The teacher will ask each new member to sign in. The session will begin with prayer.

The teacher will then pass out to each new member a copy of the lesson in the principles of salvation.[17]

The lesson will come from books by Erickson and Vangemen.[18]

The following topics will be discussed: 1) the churches view of salvation; 2) the Calvinist view; and 3) union with Christ. The teachers will discuss the principles of salvation for forty minutes. Each student will be given an opportunity to read Scriptures or related materials. The last fifteen minutes of class will be used to allow new members time to reflect. They will be asked to identify the church's view of salvation and theological doctrines of salvation, justification, glorification, regeneration, and new creation.

The new members will also be asked to characterize their union with Christ based on the work of the Son, work of the Father, and work of the Holy Spirit. At the conclusion of class, the teacher will close with a prayer. They will dismiss the class and wait an additional thirty minutes after class to answer any questions from the new members. The teachers will then turn in the sign-in sheet to the church clerk. The church clerk will maintain the class sign-in sheet to verify completion of all the classes in the Practical Foundational Principles' new member's class.

The second session will have the same setting. The teacher will open and close with prayer. They will pass out the sign-in sheet. The second session will begin with a review of the first session. The teacher will lecture on the importance of being in union with Christ for forty minutes. The last fifteen minutes of class will be used for personal reflection. The teacher will stay thirty minutes after class to answer any questions. They will turn in the sign-in sheet to the church clerk.

The disciple's prayer class will be taught in two sessions. It will cover Jesus's teachings in Matthew 6 and identify the principles of prayer using the method from PT 4572 Urban Theology class.[19]

The disciples asked Jesus how to pray, and he instructed them to pray in this manner. The class will seek to teach new members the attitude of humility and confidence in the intercessory sphere of the Holy Spirit. The teacher will begin the class with a word of prayer. They will pass out a handout depicting the lesson plan for the class. The first thirty minutes of class will be devoted to an exegesis of the Lord's Prayer in Matthew 6. The new members will be required to have a study Bible and notebook. The new member will be asked to read the Scripture and reflect on the lesson. The next fifteen minutes of class will be devoted to public prayer or intercession.

Following public prayer, the new members will discuss private prayer or self-edification. The teacher will collect the sign-in sheet and will give it to the church clerk. The teacher will remain in class an additional thirty minutes to answer questions. Session two will open with a word of prayer. The teacher will pass out the sign-in sheet. The first fifteen minutes of class will be devoted to reviewing the first session. The next thirty minutes will allow each new member two minutes to pray publicly for a current event. The final fifteen minutes of class will allow each new member an opportunity to reflect on the principle of prayer they would like to improve upon. Each new member will be asked to sign a letter of intent to participate in the weekly intercessory prayer meetings held every Wednesday. The teacher will collect both the sign-in sheet and intercessory prayer letter and turn them in to the church clerk. The teacher will remain after class for thirty minutes to answer questions.

The faith development class will be divided into two sessions. The first session will cover the stages of faith development by James W. Fowler in the book *Teaching for Spiritual Growth: An Introduction to Christian Education,* Perry G. Downs.[20]

The second session will discuss the principle of faith according to Galatians 4:1–9. The teacher will open the first session with prayer. They will pass out the sign-in sheet. The teacher would then pass out the lesson plan for the two sessions of faith development. The new members would be required to have a study Bible and notebook. If the new member does not have one, the church will provide them with one. The new member will be asked to participate in reading and class discussions. The teacher will lecture on the different stages of faith development for forty minutes. The final fifteen minutes of class will be used to allow the new members an opportunity to ask questions and give reflections on the lesson. The teacher will close the class with prayer. They will collect the sign-in sheet to forward to the church clerk. The teacher will remain thirty minutes after class to answer questions.

The second session will begin with prayer. The teacher will pass out the sign-in sheet. The first fifteen minutes of class will be used to review the different stages of faith development on a dry eraser board. The teacher will then lecture for thirty minutes on the principles of faith in Galatians 4:1–9. Galatians touches on the specific contextualization of Scripture. The new members will be instructed that not only is faith without works dead, the work of the ministry cannot save a believer. We are saved by grace through faith. A new convert is not always free from the bondage of sin. They counter their self-guilt with condemnation. Through hard work in the ministry, they feel they are decreasing the impact of the sin that so easily besets them.

The teacher will use Galatians 4 to illustrate that working does not equal discipleship. We can work in any area of ministry, but true discipleship comes from applying God's Word or principles to our lives.

For some, working in the church is their covering. Their work becomes an excuse for not participating in discipleship curriculums. It becomes an excuse as to why they do not attend formal Christian education services. It may be why their attendance barely meets the church's active membership standards (H652).[21]

During the final fifteen minutes of class, each new member will be asked to identify their stage of faith and what they need to do to reach the stage of faith consistent with their age group. The teacher will close the class with prayer. They will collect the sign-in sheet and turn it in to the church clerk.

The covenant relationship new member's class will begin with a prayer. The teacher will pass out a sign-in sheet. They will pass out the church's covenant and a handout on the covenant of grace from Gordon D. Fee's *How to Read The Bible For All Its Worth*.[22]

The class will be taught in two sessions. The new members will be required to have a study Bible and notebook. If they do not have one, the church will provide one. The first session will cover the Baptist denomination covenant agreement.

The Baptist covenant is generally read by the congregation on the first Sunday of each month, prior to partaking communion. The teacher will stress the importance of the church keeping with this covenant agreement as part of its affiliations with the Chicago Metropolitan Baptist Association, Illinois Southern Baptist Convention, and the North American Missionary Board. The first forty minutes of the class will include a lecture on the content of the churches covenant agreement. The new members will be asked to read portions of the covenant. The last fifteen minutes of class will allow the students the time to ask questions and reflect on how the Baptist denomination agrees or differs from their religious views. At the end of the first session, the teacher will collect the sign-in sheet to be turned in to the church clerk. The teacher will remain an additional thirty minutes after class to assist and answer questions. The second session will begin with prayer.

The first fifteen minutes of class will review the first session. The teacher will pass out a sign-in sheet and handout for anyone who may have missed the first session. The teacher will lecture on the six guidelines for understanding relationships by Lee.[23]

The teacher will also discuss the covenant relationships found in Genesis 15:9; Hebrews 7:22; and 2 Corinthians 3:7–18.

During the final fifteen minutes of class, the new members will be asked to identify the parallels of their own covenant agreement with God and the Baptist covenant agreement. The objective is to help each new member begin the process of adhering to the covenant of the denomination for which they have joined. In order for each new member to receive a new member's certificate, they must sign an agreement letter to live by the godly principles of the church covenant. The teacher will turn in both the sign-in sheet and agreement letter to the church clerk. The teacher will remain thirty minutes after class for additional questions.

The urban ministry class will open with prayer. The teacher will pass out the sign-in sheet. They will also pass out the class outline. The class will be divided into two sessions. The new members will be required to have a study Bible and notebook. If they do not have one, the church will provide one. A dry eraser board will be available for the teacher to make illustrations and comments.

The teacher will lecture for forty minutes on the three principles of urban ministry by Harvie M. Conn and Manuel Ortiz in the book *The Kingdom, the City & The People of God: Urban Ministry*.[24]

The three principles are servant, steward, and student. A new member will be instructed on the importance of being a servant of the Lord, a steward over all that God has given them, and becoming a life-long student on the Word of God. The last fifteen minutes of class will focus on the obstacles of ignorance that prevent community outreach. The teacher will end the class in prayer and collect the sign-in sheet. The teacher will remain after class for thirty minutes to answer questions.

Session two will begin with prayer. The teacher will pass out the sign-in sheet. The first fifteen minutes of class will be used to review the first session. The teacher will lecture for thirty minutes on Robert C. Linthicum's book, *City of God City of Satan*.[25]

The subjects will include the church's mission, the friendship corner, a call to minister, and the incarnation in the neighborhood. The last fifteen minutes of class will allow the new members time to reflect on why they joined the ministry, where they feel lead to serve, and what areas of study they would like assistance with. The church's primary purposes are discipleship, evangelism, and outreach. The new members will be asked to sign up to volunteer in one of our outreach programs. The teacher will close the class with prayer. They will collect both the sign-in sheet and volunteer sheet and turn them in to the church clerk. The teacher will remain after class an additional thirty minutes to answer questions.

The qualifications of a teacher in the new member's class is that they first complete all new member's classes. Until that time, the pastor will teach all classes. The teacher should be a good student, should be teachable, must exhibit the willingness to be open minded, should be well-versed in Scripture, able to communicate the truth of Scriptures to their students, report directly to the pastor, attend monthly teachers training, prepare weekly syllabuses for their classes, and they will inform the minister of education of any students special needs. A follow-up system to guarantee placement of volunteers should be structured. In it will be a self-discovery process. Each applicant will have a spiritual gift advisor evaluating gifts, desires, past experiences, and time schedules of each applicant. Once the applicant has committed to a ministry, a follow-up visit by the spiritual gift advisor will take place within thirty days. The follow-up visit will evaluate the progress of the applicant. They will be encouraged to continue or seek another ministry to volunteer with. Periodically, every ministries volunteer should be reevaluated. The requirement to be a teacher in the process of Christian education is for each person to have a personal relationship with God. This relationship should be based on their belief and faith in our Lord and Savior Jesus Christ.

"The things which you have heard from me in the presence of many witnesses, entrust these to faithful men who will be able to teach others also" (2 Timothy 2:2). Paul exhorts Timothy to find faithful men who were able to teach others as a requirement. A teacher should have been a good student. A person that is familiar with the challenges of learning. Good communication skills alone will not make a good Christian educator. A teacher must believe what he or she is trying to communicate. A teacher that has a relationship with the Lord based on the true principles of God's Word will be able to teach for practical, holistic, and spiritual growth. The preparation and equipping strategy in the process of the new member's class should include observation, evaluation, and changing ologies of the teachers. It is important when establishing a new member's class to include procedures for preparing and equipping potential teachers. The care of the gospel truth should supersede a desire to separate age groups. A willing person is not necessarily a qualified person. The conservative approach to education is required of a teacher.

According to Downs, "But those who are convinced of the infallibility of scripture will be able to lead others into fruitful engagement with God's word. A teacher must first be persuaded in their spirit that God's Word is true."[26]

Leadership should first observe a potential teacher. Before allowing anyone to stand before God's people and declare his truths, a person must "practice what they preach." Downs explains that it is important to first practice God's Word before teaching it.[27]

Teachers should have more experience in truth. Teaching experience in truth is more important than experience in wrong living. A student may believe that an expert in living right is a better teacher because they lived what he or she wants to live. If a crackhead feels that you have to be an ex-crack head to effectively council them, they are negating the ministry and teachings of Jesus. He was the ultimate example of a teacher. It was not necessary for Jesus to experience all of life's lows to be able to minister to that need.

Teachers should be observed based on their knowledge of Scripture.[28]

Jesus asked the religious leaders if they had read the Scriptures (Matthew 12:3, 50). Jesus wanted the religious leaders to understand that if they were going to lead God's people, they must first know the Scriptures. Jesus came to fulfill the Scripture. Their lack of knowledge hindered their acceptance of the present Messiah. Every teacher should be evaluated as often as possible. They should be evaluated to ensure compliance with the curriculum of the new member's class. The evaluation should give an accurate account of the effectiveness of the teacher's style.

It should recognize the organizational, discriminability, and readiness of both the teacher and student.[29]

The teacher is evaluated on his or her ability to organize the presentation of new information. According to Ausubel, the teacher could use three methods to make "receptive learning meaningful." The organizer assigns categories to new information. Those categories allow the student to relate the new information to existing information. The discriminability of a teacher shows his or her ability to contrast new information to existing information. A teacher should be evaluated in a classroom setting. The teacher's presentation, introduction, content, and application should be evaluated. The materials used to teach Practical Foundational Principles in the new member's class will include the creed of the church, lessons from MAUM study books, teacher's practical experience, and biblical principles of God. Each new member will receive a copy of the creed of our church. The creed represents what we as a body of Christ believe.

We believe the following truths: we believe in the triune God who exists as God the Father, the Son, and the Holy Spirit (1 John 5:7); Jesus is true God and true man (John 1:1–4); the Holy Spirit is a person in the Godhead and God's agent in the world (Romans 8); the Old and New Testament Scriptures are the divinely inspired Word of God (2 Timothy 3:16); all have sinned and come short of the glory of God and are in need of salvation (Romans 3:23); salvation has been provided for all men through the death and resurrection of Jesus Christ (Romans 10:9); it is the will of God that every believer becomes filled with the Holy Spirit (Ephesians 5:17–21); healing is provided in the redemptive work of Christ and is available to every believer (Isaiah 53:5); the ministry consists of all those who received Jesus Christ as Lord (Matthew 10:40); there shall be a bodily resurrection of the just and the unjust (1 Corinthians 15:51–58); the return of Jesus Christ will be personal and visible (1 Thessalonians 4:13–18); and we believe the doctrine of the ministry ordained by Jesus are water baptism and observance of the Lord's Supper (Acts 2:38;1 Corinthians 11:23–30).

The other materials used will come from MAUM lessons that dealt with the history of Christianity and theology.

> Christianity's roots go back into Jewish history long before the birth of Jesus Christ. It was Jesus of Nazareth, however, who attacked established Judaism and brought a renewal movement into history's light early in the first century. After his crucifixion under Pontius Pilate, a Roman official, Jesus teachings spread throughout the Mediterranean area. An apostle named Paul was especially influential. He stressed God's gift of salvation for all men and thus led in Christianity's emergence from Palestinian Judaism to a position as a universal region.[30]

Christianity dates back to the second through the eighteenth century with the fathers of the early church called patristic. Irenaeus, Aguinas, Luther, Barth, Skinner, Bloom, Gergen, and Calvin were instrumental in establishing the doctrines that shaped the creed of our local churches today. These early patriarchs dealt with the issues surrounding the image of God in historical perspective and Gnosticism.

The study of the African American church would reveal the different types of arguments or approaches used to deal with the issues of the church.[31]

The three origins are sociological, political, and anthropological. The sociological arguments dealt with racism. C. Erick Lincoln once commented that "If the black people did not exist white churches would not be necessary." To those practicing Jim Crow philosophies, white racism created the burden of segregation. The political argument dealt with self-determination. According to V. P. Franklin, the political argument was that people were for themselves, with themselves, by themselves was the attitude of African American churches. Self-determination gave way to the origin of black churches. The anthropological argument expressed the idea that churches worship the way they wanted to with the clapping of hands, songs, and dance.

It expressed the culture the way they wanted it to. The establishing of Africanism and cosmology. The new member's class will continue the process of trying to rescue the gospel message from the dominant ideology of segregation. The movement in 1963 was not about social change but a self-determination of African Americans to change the culture of America.

Major transitions in the African American church will be taught in the new member's class. The rise of black congregations such as schools, institutions, and buildings began between 1730s and 1816.[32]

During this period, there was an Angolian revival in South Carolina. The rise of black denomination and public roles of black churches took place between 1800 and 1830. The anti-slavery movement was moving across the South. By 1830s, the age of abolitionism of the black church existed. The first national Negro convention was established. There was a national shift from anti-slavery to abolitionism. The Nat Turner rebellion took place during this time. It was noted that anti-slavery suggested an inhumanity to slavery.

At the same time, abolitionist suggested that the evilness of slavery is tied to the violation of freewill. The rise of plantation missions was a direct results of white people wanting to show that they were not inhuman to people. They suggested that if African Americans were going to be Christians, then let them be one they evangelized. They tried to control evangelism and what they were talking about. The underground railroad began during that time. Nate Turner once proclaimed that the God of War is there for those who do not support peace. By 1840s, inter-racialism was contrasting with separatism. Abolitionist African Americans created black led abolitionist societies. They were questioned as to whether they should remain under the control of white abolitionist. African American abolitionist had to decide where they stood in regards to self-determination. African Americans had begun to serve as boards of trustees in the abolitionist movement. So they had already established the ability to be self-governed. In 1850s, the fugitive act on northern border churches in Canada was decimated.

By 1860s, blacks began to occupy the churches and properties in places like Tennessee and Louisiana. They began reestablishing schools. The groups of leadership were educated in the north. Educated southerners or returnees or preliterate *enslaved* African leaders. The study of theology in the Practical Foundational Principles class would include the following principles of theology natural, general, special, and the image of God. We will first consider the definition offered by Erickson:

> Theology in a Christian context is a disciple of study that seeks to understand the God revealed in the Bible and to provide a Christian understanding of reality. It seeks to understand God's creation, particularly human beings and their condition and God's redemptive work in relation to humankind. Biblical, historical, and philosophical theology provides insights and understandings that help lead toward a coherent whole. Theology has practical value in providing guidance for the Christian life and ministry.[33]

The first principle of theology is a natural theology. According to Millard J. Erickson, *Christian Theology* is a way to know God through nature, history, and human personality without the use of the Bible.[34]

He is saying that God's creation reveals rational general revelation. According to Dr. Cole in class discussion, natural theology is the knowledge of God that we can acquire with our human reason without the aid of divine revelation. In other words, what we can know about God with our Bibles shut.[35]

Thomas Aquinas, eight century, believed the two-source theory of revelation should include both revelation and natural theology. Revelation should be identified as either general or special. "All truth belongs to one of two realms."[36]

In Aquinas's view, there is a natural realm as well as a realm of grace. He concludes that human reason is qualified to understand "the existence of God's existence, immortality of the human soul, and supernatural origin of the Catholic church."[37]

The second principle of theology is general revelation. According to Erickson, general revelation is not something read into nature by those who know God on other grounds: it is already present by God's work on creation and continuing providence.[38]

General revelation according to Augustine is "from the signs of data displayed in nature, providence, and history. Common grace enables all people to intuit cognitively eternal truths concerning God's existence, character, and moral demands."[39]

John Calvin suggests that "God has given us an objective, valid, rational revelation of himself in nature, history, and human personality."[40]

The third principle of theology is special revelation. According to Erickson, special revelation is "God's manifestation of himself to particular persons at definite times and places, enabling those persons to enter into a redemptive relationship with him."[41]

The reason for a personal nature of special revelation was to renew the relationship that existed between God and his creation. Before the fall, Adam and Eve enjoyed a personal and intimate relationship with God (Genesis 2:22). We find that a special revelation goes beyond merely knowing the existence of God.

It reestablishes, "The direct presence of God, the most direct and complete form of special revelation."[42]

Exodus 3:4 gives an example of God revealing something personal about himself. He reveals to Moses that he is, "I AM That I AM" or "I will be who I will be" (Exodus 3:14, KJV). Not only did God have personal relationships with man he also established covenants with both individuals and nations.[43]

The Apostle Paul often reported personal conversations between himself and the Lord (Acts 9:4;26:14). One of the prerequisites to being an apostle of Jesus Christ was to be a witness to his resurrection.

During Paul's four missionary journeys, his desire was, "That I may know him (Christ), and the power of his resurrection, and the fellowship of his suffering, being made conformable unto his death" (Philippians 3:10, KJV). The anthropic nature of special revelation is a "revelation coming in human language and human categories of thought and action."[44]

It is often said a parable is an earthly story with a heavenly meaning. Inspired men wrote the Bible to men in a language known to its readers. God has a way of communicating his message to individuals in a way they could not be mistaken. Paul on the Damascus road in Acts 9 depicts such a case. Paul thought he was doing God's work in imprisoning and killing Christians. God took the time to visit Paul on the Damascus road. During the visit, Jesus revealed God's plan for Paul. At no time during Paul's four missionary journeys did he question God's plan for his life (Acts 20:22).

The fourth principle of theology is the study of the image of God. The image of God can be found in the study of relational, ontological, and functional concepts. The relational shows how male and female constitutes image of God. Ontological reveals the essential nature of something. Functional depicts man's job description.

Christological is the study of Christ. "Human beings are created for life in relationships that mirror or correspond to God's own life in relationship."[45]

According to Migliore male and female constitute the image of God. The Scripture reference is Genesis 1:26–27. We find that "God created man in His own image, in the image of God He created him; male and female He created them" (Genesis 1:27, NASB).

Just as God has a relationship with the Son (Jesus) and the Holy Spirit, mankind establishes a relationship with God and one another. How we deal with one another should mirror the trinity and unity God has with both his Son and Spirit. The ontological concept represents the essential nature of something. Migliore gave three examples of ontological aspect of the image of God: rationality, volatility, and moral sense.[46]

The pastor and teachers of the new member's class will evaluate the project. Evaluations will be accomplished using evaluation forms. There will be monthly teachers meetings to evaluate the effectiveness of the curriculum. There will be attention given to the transformation of the new members. The discipline and service of the new members will be monitored. The teachers will be evaluated based on their presentation, deliverance, and practical application of each lesson. The new members will be evaluated based on their attendance, participation, and spiritual growth. The new members that signed up for intercessory prayer meetings, covenant agreement letter, and outreach volunteer sheet will be monitored. The objective is to educate new members about church doctrine and fellowship. Once the new members have received the foundational materials from the new member's class their service, stewardship and biblical studies will be evaluated.

New Member Class Survey

I. Basic Church Information

Church name: _____

Street Address: _____

City: _____ State:_____ Zip:_____

Phone: (day) (___) _____(evening) (___)_____

Fax (if applicable): (___)_____

Email:_____

Age of the church (number of years the church has been in existence as a constituted body): _____Years _____Months

Name of person completing this survey: _____

Position held in the church: _____

Phone (if needed to clarify response): (___)_____

Email:_____

Does your church currently have a new member class? ___Yes ___No

If your response to the previous question is "No," complete 3 only section I and II, and then return the survey to sender. All others should respond to the rest of the survey.

A. Please us the information from your annual church profile or your church minutes to complete the following information. If your church does not keep records for the following categories, please mark N/A.

    1. Regular membership_____
    2. Average morning worship attendance_____
    3. Average Sunday School attendance_____
    4. Total additions by conversion (Baptism)_____
    5. Total additions by transfer of membership_____
    6. Total of *all* additions_____

B. Please provide the following geographic and demographic information about the church.

    7. Church setting:

        _____a. Open country/rural area
        _____b. Town (500) to 2,499 people)
        _____c. Small city (2,500 to 9,999 people)
        _____d. Medium city/downtown (10,000 to 49,999 people)
        _____e. Medium city/suburbs (10,000 to 49,999 people)
        _____f. Large city/downtown or inner city (50,000 + people)
        _____g. Large city/suburbs (50,000 + people)

    8. Congregational demographics of active membership

Race	*Age*	*Economic Levels*
Caucasian ____%	Under 18 ___%	Upper class ___%
African American ___%	19–35 ___%	Middle class ___%
Hispanic ___%	36–50___%	Lower class___%
Asian ____%	51–65___%	
Other___%	66+ ___%	

II. *Church Staff Information*

9. Senior pastor's name:_____
10. Senior pastor's highest education level:

    _____a. High School   _____c. Seminary (master's degree)
    _____b. College   _____d. Seminary (doctorate)
    _____e. Seminary studies (no degree)

11. Is the senior pastor full-time? _____Yes _____No
12. How long has the senior pastor served at the church?
    _____years _____months
13. Which other paid staff positions does the church have?

    _____a. Associate Pastor
    _____b. Minister of music/worship
    _____c. Minister of Education
    _____d. Minister of youth/students
    _____e. Others

III. *New Member's Class Information*

14. How long has the church had a new member class?
    _____years _____months
15. Please list any obstacles the church faced in establishing a new member class (e.g., opposition from leaders, questions about who should attend)
16. Does your church require or expect new members to attend a new member's course?
    _____Require _____Expect _____Neither
17. What does your church call the new member class (what name do you use for the course)?

    _____

18. If you require a new member class, must the course be completed before new members are accepted into the church? _____Yes _____No _____N/A

19. Are prospects and visitors permitted and/or encouraged to attend the new member/orientation course? _____Permitted _____Encouraged _____Neither (Class is reserved for new members.)

20. Using the following scale, indicate the purpose(s) of your new member class.

1	2	3	4	5
Not at all		Somewhat		A Primary
A purpose		a purpose		purpose

_____a. providing orientation to the church in general

_____b. teaching about the church's basic doctrine

_____c. building relationships among new members

_____d. introducing class members to the church staff

_____e. offering opportunities for new members to get involved in the ministry of the church

_____f. carrying out evangelism—sharing the gospel with class members

_____g. other:_____

21. Who teaches the new member class?

_____a. Senior pastor   _____c. Layperson
_____b. Staff member   _____d. Other

22. When does the new member course meet?
Day(s)_____ Time:_____ # of sessions_____

23. How often is the course offered? _____

24. Does the class meet _____ at the church or _____ away from church?

25. Which of the following topics are addressed in the new member class. Please mark all that apply.

_____a. Doctrine of the church
_____b. Polity and government of your church
_____c. History of your church
_____d. Requirements for membership
_____e. Expectations of members after joining
_____f. Policies for disciplining/excluding members
_____g. Training for witnessing/evangelism
_____h. Training in spiritual disciplines (prayer, study, etc.)
_____i. Plan of salvation
_____j. Examination of the church covenant
_____k. Inventory of spiritual gifts
_____l. Explanation of the church's mission and/or vision
_____m. Structure, history, and polity of the denomination
_____n. Introductions to church staff and leadership
_____o. Current opportunities for service in the church
_____p. Tithing/financial support of the church
_____q. Examination of church constitution
_____r. Structure/support of missions through the Cooperative Program or other denominational programs
_____s. Method and meaning of Baptism
_____t. Purpose of the Lord's Supper
_____u. Tour of the church facilities
_____v. Other:_____

26. Does your church use a specific book, study guide, or kit for the new member class, what resource(s) do you use? Please be specific. If you have produced your own materials, would you please send us a copy?

27. Do you have an established means by which you evaluate the new member class?
_____Yes _____No _____N/A

28. If you do evaluate the class, how do you do so?
29. What percentage of members who have joined within the past two years attended a new member class? _____%
30. What percentage of members who have joined within the last two years are currently active in the church (attending worship at least twice a month and involved in some other type of activity or ministry in the church)? _____%
31. What percentage of your current active members have completed a new member class at your church? _____%
32. What *one* change would you like to see made in the church's new member's class?
33. Many church leaders ask the question, "If we begin a new member's class, should the long-term members be expected or required to take it?" How does your church address this important question?

Please include with your responses any outlines, curriculum, materials, etc., you use that may help us better understand your church's new member class.

Please return this survey and any other information which might assist us in implementing a new member's class. Thank you for your assistance with this study.

PRACTICAL WORD MINISTRIES

The Vision

> And the Lord answered me, and said, "Write the vision, and make it plain upon tables, that he may run that readeth it. For the vision if yet for an appointed time, but at the end it shall speak, and not lie: though it tarry, wait for it; because it will surely come, it will not tarry." (Habakkuk 2:2–3, KJV)

Practical Word Ministries is a non-profit Southern Baptist organization. Its mission is to reach all ethnic backgrounds, minister to the spiritual and social needs of our community, nurture the faith in our youth, and minister on the principle that the practical application of the Word of God changes lives.

Step 1: Purchase our own facility for multipurpose uses. It will be a worship center; fellowship hall; and outreach center. It should be at least 2,000 sq. feet in size. After we build the Lord a house, the facility will be renamed *The Friendship Corner*.

Step 2: Open a breakfast and lunch *restaurant*. Members of Practical Word Ministry will staff the restaurant. The manager will have received their food sanitation certificate from the City of Chicago. Practical Word will assist any member in good standing in getting the appropriate training.

Step 3: Enlarge the *landscape service* business. The landscape crew will be members of Practical Word Ministries. The supervisors will have driver's license. This will be a seasonal job lasting from spring through the fall.

Step 4: Christian *barbershop*. The barbershop manager and all stylists will have been licensed by the state of Illinois. Practical Word will assist any member in good standing in obtaining the appropriate training.

Step 5: Low income *housing*. Practical Word Ministries will purchase two flat and three flat buildings to be converted to either two apartment or rooming houses. The general contractors of Practical Word will perform the construction and maintenance of properties.

B. Evaluation

The first objective of Practical Foundational Principles, new member's class, is to prepare new members with the foundational skills necessary to become functional members of a local church and body of Christ. Dysfunctional families and relationships are rampant in homes all over the country and state. The majority of children have grown up in a single-parent environment. The father is either in jail or on drugs. The mother has to be the disciplinarian. Or the mother is on drugs and has abandoned her children. There are abandoned children in DCFS. These children have conflicts as they grow older with their identity. The Practical Foundational Principles new member's class will seek to direct the new convert to their identity in Christ. The foundational skills will begin with the understanding and study of the creed of the local church.

The Practical Foundational Principles, new member's class at Practical Word Ministries located at 9521 S. LaSalle, Chicago, Illinois, began at 1:00 p.m. on Sunday January 31, 2010. The pastor was the teacher. The classroom was set up according to the method in a project design format. The teacher passed out the sign-in sheet. The sign-in sheet was would be collected fifteen minutes from the start of class. Anyone entering the class after the first fifteen minutes would not receive credit for the session. The teacher explained that there would be five classes with each class having two sessions. The classes included following syllabus: principles of salvation, disciples prayer, faith development, covenant relationships, and urban ministry. The Practical Foundational Principles class would conclude with the new members completing a class survey.

A new member opened the class with a word of prayer. The teacher then passed out the principles of salvation outline for the next two sessions. The first fifteen minutes of class was dedicated to introducing the new member's class, its curriculum, and participant's requirements. A notebook was provided to the new members for a record of reflections and additional notes.

The teacher began lecturing on the church's view of salvation using Romans 3:23;10:9;Acts 4:12;and Milard J. Erickson's *Christian Theology, Second Edition*. The class discussed the Calvinist view of salvation. During class, the new members read Scriptures and notes from the outline. They participated in answering questions about the doctrine of salvation. They took reflective notes. The new members were asked to reflect on their union with Christ from Willem Vargenern's *The Progress of Redemption: The Story of Salvation from Creation to the New Jerusalem*. The teacher concluded the class at 2:30 p.m. with a word of prayer. The teacher remained an additional thirty minutes after class to answer questions. The sign-in sheet was forwarded to the church clerk.

The second session on the principles of salvation class began with a word of prayer by a new member. There were four new members present. The teacher passed out the sign-in sheet and class outline for those who missed the first session. The class spent the first fifteen minutes of class reviewing key topics in the first session. The teacher began lecturing on the union with Christ through the work of the spirit. It becomes evident after forty-five minutes into the class that one hour was not sufficient enough. The studies scheduled for the second session were condensed to fit the time restraints. The class spent the last fifteen minutes of class reviewing the judicial, spiritual, and vital aspects of being in union with Christ. Each new member was asked to reflect on their perceived union with Christ based on the work of the Son, Father, and Holy Spirit. The doctrine concerning salvation was re-emphasized. It was determined that one hour does not give sufficient time for class participation and reflection. Therefore, the classes will be extended by one hour to two hours long per session. The class will be from 1:30 p.m. to 3:30 p.m. The sign-in sheet was turned in to the church clerk. The teacher remained thirty minutes after class to answer questions.

The first session of the disciple's prayer class began with a word of prayer. The sign-in sheet was passed around class. The outline of the class was given to each new member. There were five new members in class. Previous classes were too short to cover all the required materials. This class was scheduled for two hours instead of the previous one-hour method. The class began with a brief review of the outline. There was a one-hour lecture on the exegesis of the Lord's Prayer in Matthew 6:9–13. The Lord's Prayer was meant as a disciple's prayer. A disciple or learner understands the significance of the manner of prayer prescribed by Jesus. He suggests that our prayer include exaltation will provision, repentance, and guidance. The class spent fifteen minutes discussing the attitude of humility as taught in Scriptures. The final fifteen minutes of class considered the confidence in the intercessory sphere of the Holy Spirit. The class was asked to reflect on prayer as being momentary. For every opportunity to pray must consider the moment in time that the prayer is offered. The class concluded at 2:30 p.m. The teacher closed the class with a word of prayer. The sign-in sheet was forwarded to the church clerk. The teacher remained an additional thirty minutes after class to answer questions.

Session two of disciple prayer began with prayer by a new member. There were seven new members present. The sign-in sheet was passed out. The outline of the class was distributed. The class began with an overview of session one for fifteen minutes. The confidence in the intercessory sphere of the Holy Spirit from 1 Corinthians 2:9–16 was discussed. We recognized that the Holy Spirit leads a believer in knowing what to pray and how to pray. We also concluded that we pray in the moment each time we pray. The class spent thirty minutes discussing public prayer or intercession using Ezekiel 22:30, Romans 8:26, and James 5:16. Thirty minutes was dedicated to private prayer of self-edification using Matthew 26:41 and Proverbs 15:29. Fifteen minutes was spent allowing each new member to pray over current events such as infirmities, unemployment, foreclosure, incarceration, Haiti earthquake, youth, and education. The new members were given time to reflect on their personal prayer life. One member indicated they were not comfortable praying privately or publicly due to past transgressions. The class discussed Romans 12:10. A letter of intent to participate in weekly prayer meetings was passed out in class. Six new members signed up for the weekly prayer meeting. The sign-in sheet and letter of intent was given to the church clerk. The teacher closed the class with a word of prayer. The teacher remained an additional thirty minutes after class to answer questions.

Session one of faith development in new member's class began with a word of prayer from a new member. There were six new members present. The class began at 1:30 p.m.

Sunday, February 28, 2010. The sign-in sheet was passed around the class. The class outline and notebooks were distributed to the new members. The teacher lectured for one hour on the six stages of faith development by James W. Fowler in *Teaching For Spiritual Growth: An Introduction to Christian Education* by Perry G. Downs. Stage one is the intuitive/projective faith (two to six years of age). During this phase, there is magical thinking. They are influenced by images, stories, and symbols. Stage two is a mythical/literal faith (six to twelve years of age). This stage is when someone is generally limited to concrete thinking. They are unable to see spiritual realities or respond to biblical truths. Stage three is a synthetic/conventional faith (thirteen to eighteen years of age). They see themselves in relation to others. They adopt the belief systems and forms of a larger community. Stage four is individuative/reflective faith (nineteen to forty years of age). They begin to make choices based solely on the self apart from the group. This stage also asks why the group believes and acts as it does. Stage five is the conjunctive faith (forty one and beyond age groups). During this stage of faith, a person becomes aware of their own limitations. They have a new sense of humility. Stage six is the universalizing faith (midlife and beyond age groups). They have a new identification with the work of God and his kingdom. They are also conscious of transformation into the image of Jesus. The class spent thirty minutes discussing questions and personal reflections. The sign-in sheet was turned to the teacher. The class ended with a word of prayer. The sign-in sheet was given to the church clerk. The teacher remained an additional thirty minutes to answer questions.

Session two of the faith development class began with a new member giving a word of prayer. There were four new members present. The teacher passed out the sign-in sheet and the outline for those who missed session one. The first fifteen minutes of class allowed time to review the six stages of faith development from session one. The teacher then lectured on the principles of faith using Galatians 4:1–9. The class spent forty minutes exegesis those Scriptures. The principle theme was working does not equal discipleship. Following the lecture, the class spent thirty minutes allowing each new member an opportunity to identify their individual stage of faith. Each new member reflected on the contrast between Fowler's theory of faith development and how it applied to their spiritual journey. The new member then expounded on what stage of faith should reflect their spiritual journey. The teacher collected the sign-in sheet and gave it to the church clerk. The teacher remained an additional thirty minutes after class to answer any questions.

Session one of covenant relationship class began with a word of prayer by a new member. There were four new members present. The teacher passed around the sign-in sheet. The teacher passed out the class outline. A Bible and notebook was given to new member students as needed. The first forty minutes of class covered the purpose, definition, Baptist covenant agreement, church affiliations, and new member's views. Each new member was given an opportunity to read and reflect on the importance of keeping the covenant. Emphasis was placed on the economic impact of keeping a covenant agreement with their local church. The church affiliations included Chicago Metropolitan Baptist Association (CMBA). The CMBA provides the church with administrative assistance and pastoral fellowship with the African Americans Southern Baptist Fellowship. The Illinois

Baptist State Association (ISBA) which enables the church to have a 501c (3) tax exempt status. It also provides a monthly new letter for all Southern Baptist churches in the State of Illinois. The North American Missionary Baptist (NAMB). The NAMB provides monetary assistance with the church's Hunger program. The hunger program distributes ten tons of food and clothing annually to the needy. It also allows the church to get involved with international ministry. Through the cooperative fund, we donate money toward missionaries in places like China, Haiti, and Sudan. The class concluded with a fifteen-minute discussion on how the Baptist denomination agrees or differ from their religious views. The class ended with a closing prayer by the teacher. The teacher collected the sign-in sheet and forwarded to the church clerk. The teacher remained an additional thirty minutes after class to answer questions.

Session two of the covenant relationship class began with the teacher passing out the sign-in sheet and outline. There were six new members in attendance. The first fifteen minutes of class was dedicated to reviewing session one. The next forty five minutes of class involved a lecture on the six guidelines for understanding the relationship of the Christian to the Old Testament Law from Fee. The class then discussed covenant relationships in Genesis 15:9, Hebrews 7:22, and 2 Corinthians 3:7–18. The new members were given an opportunity to show parallels of their own covenant agreement with God and Baptist covenant agreement. The final fifteen minutes of class allowed the students' time to reflect on both sessions and sign a letter of agreement to keep the church covenant. The class ended with a prayer by the teacher. The teacher collected the sign-in sheet and agreement letter to forward to the church clerk. The teacher remained an additional thirty minutes to answer questions.

The first session of the Urban Ministry class began with an opening prayer by a new member. The teacher passed out the sign-in sheet and class outline. There were five new members in attendance. The teacher ensured that all new members had a Bible and notebook. The first forty minutes of class was a lecture on the Three Principles of Urban Ministry by Harvie M. Conn and Manuel Ortiz. The first principle was becoming a servant of the Lord in humility, service to others, and a character of a servant. The second principle was being a steward over all that God has given us by managing the house for the owner, must be able to teach, and apply the Word of God holistically. The third principle was becoming a student, life-long student of the Word of God. The class concluded with a thirty-minute discussion on the obstacles of ignorance that prevents community outreach. The teacher collected the sign-in sheet. The teacher closed the class with a word of prayer. The teacher remained thirty minutes after class to answer questions. The teacher forwarded the sign-in sheet to the church clerk.

Session two of the Urban Ministry class began with a new member giving a word of prayer. The teacher passed out the sign-in sheet and outline. The first fifteen minutes of class were spent reviewing session one. The teacher lectured for thirty minutes on Robert C. Linthicum's book *City of God City of Satan*. The lecture considered what Jesus had done for the city and the salvation for a city. The class spent thirty minutes reviewing the church's mission, the Friendship Corner, a call to ministry, and incarnation in the neighborhood. The final fifteen minutes of class allowed the new members an opportunity to sign an outreach program volunteer letter. The teacher collected the sign-in sheet and outreach program volunteer letter to be forwarded to church clerk. The teacher remained thirty minutes after class for reflections and to answer questions.

C. What I Learned

The Practical Foundational Principles, new member's class, taught me the importance of teacher preparedness. Each class produced an atmosphere of reflections and convictions that required scriptural insights. The new members came with certain expectations to learn more about the ministry and themselves. As the teacher of each class, I was challenged to not only teach but also pull the best out of each new member. It is one thing to lecture. It is another to draw men and women into dialogue that causes them to reflect and respond to their spiritual journey.

Each class provided its own elements of illumination to Scripture and personal realization. Let's consider what classes brought out in the lives of the new members. The principles of salvation introduced the new members to the idea of being in union with Christ judicially, spiritually, and vitally. I learned that new converts and some elderly Christians are not aware of the significance of being in union with Christ. The disciples' prayer class challenged the new members to consider their personal prayer life. While one new member showed a reluctance to pray openly another prayed in confidence. The faith development class allowed the new members an opportunity to reflect on their individual level of faith. I learned that adults could remain in the faith level of children. The covenant relationship class revealed the responsibilities of individual members to their local church and the church's responsibility to its affiliates. I learned that most new members think a church exit in isolation. They may not realize the importance of covenant relationships or its impact on the local church. And finally, the urban ministry class revealed the voluntarism of the outreach ministry at the local church. I learned that evangelism is not a given. It is something that has to be taught as well as illustrated to new converts. Our ministry requires a great deal of evangelism. We were challenged with persuading individual new members to participate in an outreach ministry that will take them out of their comfort zones.

D. Recommendations to Improve

The major recommendation to improve the Practical Foundational Principles' new member's class would be the time restraints. Each class began as a one-hour session. One hour after the morning worship service on the surface appears to be a long time. However, when engulfed in the atmosphere of both teaching and learning an hour is a short time. The class lengths should change from one hour to a maximum of two hours. The first hour normally would involve an introduction to the class syllabus. That would be followed by a lecture on the main discourse of the principle of the class. Time should be allocated for questions and reflections. If I have learned anything from my eight years as a Reach student, it is that adults respond well to participation in class. This requires at least forty minutes for arguments and reflections.

Another recommendation to improve in the class would be the ability to have the new members begin participating in the local ministry after signing a letter of intent. Each new member was given an opportunity to sign letters of intent in the winter season. The ministries they consented to participate in were not being offered at the time such as intercessory prayer on Wednesday, fellowshipping with affiliations, outreach ministries of food, and cloth drives. Although each class produced spiritual growth in the new members, both learning and practical application would have yielded a result in each new member that would enhance their ability to remain a functional member of the body of Christ.

APPENDICES

Practical Word Ministries

"For he hath made him to be sin for us who knew no sin, that we might be made the righteousness of God in him" (Corinthians 25:24).

Foundation Class #1	Principles of Salvation 1
Matthew 3:1–2	Repent ye (Jesus).
Acts 2:38	Repent all of you (Peter).
	Repent turning away from your own ability.
	Repent is a godly sorrow.
1 John 1:9	If we confess our sins, He is faithful and just to forgive us and clean us from all unrighteous.
Roman 3:23	For all have sinned and come short of the glory of God.
John 8:44	Nature of sin: Before you got saved.
John 3:3	You must be born again.
John 10:10	The thief cometh not but to steal, kill and destroy.
2 Corinthians 5:17	Therefore if any man be in Christ, he is a new creature.

Memory Verses
Ephesians 2:8–9
Galatians 2:20
Romans 3:23

Practical Word Ministries
Foundation Class #2   Principles of Salvation 2

Acts 16:25–29   Paul and Silas imprisoned.
Hebrews 11:1   By faith.
Colossians 2:12–15   Buried with him in baptism.
Galatians 3:13–15:29
John 14:26–27
Acts 2:1–7
Ephesians 1:4

Memory Verses
Acts 2:38
Acts 4:12
2 Corinthians 5:17

Practical Word Ministries
Foundation Class #3   Disciples' Prayer

1 Corinthians 2:9–16   Intercessory sphere of the Holy Spirit.
                       Pray in the moment.
Ezekiel 22:30   Public prayer.
Romans 8:26
James 5:16
Matthew 26:4   Self-edification.

Proverbs 15:29
Romans 12:10

Memory Verses
  Romans 8:26
  James 5:16
  Proverbs 15:29

Practical Word Ministries
  Foundation Class #4   Disciples' Prayer

  Matthew 21: 12–17
  Luke 11:1   Jesus teaches the disciples how to pray.
  Luke 9:51–56
  Ephesians 6:12–18
  Psalm 100:1–5
  Acts 15:25–31   Paul and Silas.
  Matthew 18:19
  Philippians 4:6
  John 15:7–16
  Ezekiel 22:30   Stand in the gap.

Memory Verses
  Ezekiel 22:30
  Luke 10:10
  Philippians 4:6

Practical Word Ministries
    Foundation Class #5   Faith Development

Hebrews 11:1	Faith
Romans 10:17	How to get faith.
Romans 10:10	
Mark 11:11–20	The fruitless fig tree. Speak the Word and Release the Word of faith.
Acts 14:7	Lystra impotent on his feet, being a cripple from his mother's womb.
John 20:29	
Mark 9:23	
James 2:20	
Hebrews 6:12	
2 Kings 6:5	

Memory verses
    Hebrews 11:1
    Hebrews 11:6
    Romans 10:17

Practical Word Ministries
    Foundation Class #6   Covenant Relationships

Genesis 12:1–3	
Genesis 17:1–12	
Genesis 24:35, 26:3,12,15,18	
1 Samuel 17:26–45	David and Goliath.
1 Samuel 14:6	Jonathan's daring attack.
Mark 4:35–40	Peace Be Still.

Galatians 3:13–14, 27, 28, 29	Redeemed us from the curse.
Isaiah 53:5	
Matthew 28:20	
2 Corinthians 5:21	
Philippians 4:19	

Memory Verses
2 Corinthians 5:21
Galatians 3:13–14
Psalm 91:1–5

Practical Word Ministries

Foundation Class #7	Healing
Psalm 103:3	Who healed all thy diseases…
Exodus 15:26	
Acts 10:38	God is not holding back.
Ephesians 1:3	
1 Peter 2:24	…by whose strips ye were healed.
Mark 1:40	Jesus cleanses a leper, His will.
Mark 5:34	His way.
Luke 13:12	Healing a crippled woman.
Romans 4:17	Call upon those things which be not as though they were…
Matthew 8:17	How do we receive? (Study, mediate, and confess).

Memory Verses
1 Peter 2:24
John 10:10
Romans 8:11

Practical Word Ministries

    Foundation Class #8   Prosperity

    Psalm 24:1   God owns it all.
    Haggai 2:8
    Psalm 50:10
    Proverbs 13:22   Made us stewards.
    Mark 10:21
    Genesis 12:1–3, 13:2
    1 Timothy 6:17–18
    Deuteronomy 8:18
    1 Timothy 6:10   What our attitude should be like.
    Genesis 12:2
    Malachi 3:10   God is your source.
    2 Corinthians 9:6
    Galatians 3:13–14
    Philippians 4:19

Memory Verses

    2 Corinthians 9:6
    3 John 1:2
    Psalm 35:27

Practical Word Ministries

    Foundation Class #9   Righteousness

    2 Corinthians 5:21   What is righteousness? It is no goodie, goodie. It is the nature of God.
    1 John 4:4   No sense of inferiority (lack failure).
    2 Corinthians 5:21   How did we become his righteousness? Jesus was made sin for us.

John 17:16
Romans 3:22–24   By faith in Jesus.
Psalm 34:17   How does it affect our life?
James 5:16

Memory Verses
2 Corinthians 5:21
1 John 4:4
Romans 5:17

Practical Word Ministries
Foundation Class #10   Evangelism

Mark 16:15   The Commission. "Go ye…"
Hebrews 4:12   The ability. "For the Word of God is quick (alive…)."
Acts 1:8   …But ye shall receive power after the Holy Ghost is come upon you.
Romans 3:23   The decision.
Romans 6:23
2 Corinthians 5:21
John 12:47   Not to judge.
John 12:45
John 4:4   The woman of Samaria.

Memory Verses
Romans 3:23
Romans 6:23
2 Corinthians 5:17

NOTES

1. Perry G. Downs, *Teaching For Spiritual Growth.* p. 49.
2. John Conaway, Steve Wamberg, *Faith Teaching: Teachers Like You Can Grow Faith Kids.* p. 19.
3. Downs, p. 19.
4. Ibid., p. 60.
5. Ibid., p. 24.
6. Ibid., p. 200.
7. Downs, p. 64.
8. Millard J. Erickson, *Christian Theology.* p. 177.
9. Michael D. Reynolds, class notes of student in PT 601, Urban Church Education, Trinity Evangelical Seminary, Spring 2007.
10. City-Data.Com, 60628 Zip Code Detailed Profile. p. 1.
11. Bruce L. Fields, class notes of student in ST 5103, Holy Spirit, Church and Last Things, Trinity Evangelical Seminary, Fall 2007.
12. Perry G. Downs, class notes of student in EM 501, Urban Educational Ministry of the Church, Trinity Evangelical Seminary, Spring 2006.
13. Michael D. Reynolds, class notes of student in PT 602, Urban Ministry Practicum, Trinity Evangelical Seminary, Winter 2007.
14. McRobert, Four Corners. p. 82.
15. Ibid., p. 83.
16. Perry G. Downs, class notes of student in EM 501, Urban Educational Ministry of the Church, Trinity Evangelical Seminary, Spring 2006.
17. Erickson, p. 958.
18. William Vangemeren, *The Progress of Redemption: The Story of Salvation from Creation to the New Jerusalem.* p. 404.
19. Dr. Michael D. Reynolds, class notes of student in PT 4572, Urban Theology, Trinity Evangelical Seminary, Fall 2007.
20. Downs, p. 114.

21. Dr. Michael D. Reynolds, class notes of student in H 652, Hermeneutic and Homiletic, Trinity Evangelical Seminary, winter 2007. 22 Gordon D. Fee, How to Read The Bible for All Its Worth. p. 165.

22. Gordon D. Fee, How to Read The Bible for All Its Worth. p. 165.

23. Ibid., p. 166.

24. Harvie M. Conn and Manuel Ortiz, The Kingdom, the City & the People of God: Urban ministry. p. 403.

25. Robert C. Linthicum, City of God City of Satan. p. 111.

26. Carl F. George, Robert E. Logan, *Leading & Managing Your Church*. p. 36.

27. Ibid., p. 26.

28. Ibid., p. 41.

29. Ibid., p. 176.

30. Bruce L. Shelley, *Church History in Plain Language*. p. 1.

31. David D. Daniels, class notes of student in CH 675, The Black Church in North America, Trinity Evangelical Seminary, Spring 2009.

32. Ibid., Spring 2009.

33. Erickson, p. 17.

34. Ibid., p. 181.

35. Graham A. Cole, class notes of student in ST 5102, Christ, Sin, and Salvation, Trinity Evangelical Seminary, Spring 2008.

36. Erickson, p. 181.

37. Ibid., p. 182.

38. Erickson, p. 195.

39. Bruce A. DeMarest, *General Revelation: Historical Views and Contemporary Issues*. p. 28.

40. Erickson, p. 194.

41. Ibid., p. 201.

42. Ibid., p. 202.

43. Ibid., p. 203.

44. Ibid., p. 204.

45. Daniel L. Migliore, *Faith Seeking Understanding: An Introduction to Christian Theology*. p. 141.

46. Ibid., p. 140.

BIBLIOGRAPHY

Books

Conaway, John Wamberg, Steve. *Faith Teaching: Teachers Like You Can Grow Faith Kids*. Cook: USA, 1999.

DeMarest Bruce A. *General Revelation: Historical Views and Contemporary Issues*. Zondervan: Grand Rapids, 1982.

Downs, Perry G. *Teaching for Spiritual Growth: An Introduction to Christian Education*. Zondervan: Grand Rapids, 1994.

Erickson, Millard J. *Christian Theology*. Blackwell: Oxford, 1995.

George, Carl F. Logan, Robert E. *Leading & Managing Your Church*. Fleming H. Revel: Grand Rapids, 1982.

McRoberts, Omar M. Streets of Glory: *Church and Community in a Black Urban Neighborhood*. University of Chicago: Chicago, 2003.

Migliore, Daniel L. *Faith Seeking Understanding: An Introduction to Christian Theology*. Wm. B. Eerdmais: Grand Rapids, 2004.

Shelley, Bruce L. *Church History in Plain Language*. Word: Nelson, 1982.

Vangemeren, William. *The Progress of Redemption: The Story of Salvation from Creation to the New Jerusalem*. Baker: Grand Rapids, 1988.

Bible, Commentaries, Dictionary, and Periodical

New American Standard Bible. Zondervan: Grand Rapids, 2002. The Holy Bible. World: Iowa Falls, 75m-6-86.

Vine, W.E. Unger, Merrill F. White, William Jr. VINE'S Complete Expository Dictionary of Old and New Testament Words. Thomas Nelson: Nashville, 1985.

Unpublished Materials

Cole, Graham A. class notes of student in ST 5102, Christ, Sin, Man and Salvation, Trinity Evangelical Seminary, Spring 2008.

Daniels, David D. class notes of student in CH 675, The Black Church in North America, Trinity Evangelical Seminary, Spring 2009.

Downs, Perry G. class notes of student in EM 501, Urban Educational Ministry of the Church, Trinity Evangelical Seminary, Spring 2006.

Fields, Bruce L. class notes of student in ST 5103, Holy Spirit, church and Last Things, Trinity Evangelical Seminary, Fall 2007.

Greene, Madeline C. class notes of student in PT 7471, Project Design, Trinity Evangelical Seminary, Fall 2009.

Reynolds, Michael D. class notes of student in PT 601, Urban Church Education, Trinity Evangelical Seminary, Spring 2007.

Reynolds, Michael D. class notes of student in PT 602, Urban Ministry Practicum, Trinity Evangelical Seminary, Winter 2007.

Websites

Ccel. Org. Aquinas. (2008), from www.ccel.org/ecel/aquinas/summa.fp.ix.fp_q93_al.html.

City-Data. Com, 60628 Zip Code Detailed Profile. Retrieved December 4, 2008, from www.shilohmbc.com.

ABOUT THE AUTHOR

Franklin L. Elmore, a theology graduate of Trinity International Divinity School in 2010, accepted his calling to preach the gospel of Jesus Christ in the fall of 1989 while serving in the United States Air Force.

He grew up the twelfth child of a former share cropper from Clarksdale Mississippi. Living in project housing until graduating from high school at Paducah Tilghman High School in Paducah Kentucky, he was baptized at an early age in 1969 as a member of Ninth Street Tabernacle Baptist Church in lower town. With only one significant emotional feeling, he really never had a relationship with the Lord.

After joining the Armed Forces in 1979 until 1989, he became very worldly. He stopped going to church. At one point in his prodigal son's experience, he told a young man to stop talking about Jesus because it offended him. Never really having spiritual life, he drifted from one disappointment to the next. Early one Monday morning in November of 1989, he was born again. He received a visitation from Jesus Christ as his Lord and Savior.

Since that time, he has dedicated his life to his strongest conviction, fulfilling his calling to preach the gospel. He served as associate minister for over nine years at various ministries. The Lord blessed Franklin with a beautiful Christian wife, Arnetha Walker; three sons Kemonte, Larance, Michael; and seven grandchildren.

While attending undergraduate college at Trinity International University in 2005, he was led to incorporate his personal ministry under the name of Practical Word Ministries Inc. in Chicago, Illinois. He became affiliated with Southern Baptist Conference. With the help of Hands of Hope Ministry in Joilet, Illinois, and The Southern Baptist Hunger Programs, the ministry served hot meals and distributed tons of food and clothing in the Roseland community on the south side. The outreach ministry was called The Friendship Corner.

During Sunday morning worship services, a speaker was placed on the outside of the building located at 150 West 95th Street. The gangs, alcoholics, drug addicts, and prostitutes heard the Word of the Lord. He still ministers in the Dolton, Illinois, area. The Word of God is still changing lives.

CPSIA information can be obtained
at www.ICGtesting.com
Printed in the USA
BVHW080755261021
619846BV00005B/298

9 781098 010188